Willard Daniel Johnson

Outlines of the History of Education

For teachers' training classes and all who desire an elementary knowledge

of the subject

Willard Daniel Johnson

Outlines of the History of Education
For teachers' training classes and all who desire an elementary knowledge of the subject

ISBN/EAN: 9783337248222

Printed in Europe, USA, Canada, Australia, Japan

Cover: Foto ©Paul-Georg Meister /pixelio.de

More available books at **www.hansebooks.com**

OUTLINES

OF THE

HISTORY OF EDUCATION,

FOR

TEACHERS' TRAINING CLASSES

AND ALL WHO DESIRE AN ELEMENTARY KNOWL-
EDGE OF THE SUBJECT.

BY

W. D. JOHNSON, PH. M.

PRINCIPAL OF THE COOPERSTOWN HIGH SCHOOL.

1899
CRIST, SCOTT & PARSHALL, PUBLISHERS.
COOPERSTOWN, N. Y.

Entered, according to act of Congress, in the year eighteen hundred and ninety-nine,
By CRIST, SCOTT & PARSHALL,
In the Office of the Librarian of Congress, at Washington.

TWO COPIES RECEIVED.

PREFACE.

When called upon to instruct a class in the history of education in a New York State training class, I could find no book covering all requirements in the subject by the Department of Public Instruction. I found many books which contain satisfactory information on many topics in the training class syllabus, while some topics could be found discussed in the largest encyclopedias, only.

When the pupil prepared his lessons from these numerous and exhaustive treatises, he often wasted time by reading much not essential and often failed to understand what he read. After three years of careful reading, I have succeeded in compiling notes on the subject for my class. These notes were dictated to my last class. The final examination was readily passed. Believing from this experience and from the expressions of other teachers of training classes that these notes may be of service to other pupils, I venture to have the notes published.

It is the wish of the author that this volume may be received in the spirit in which it is sent out. The book is intended to be a guide, only, to the study of the history of education.

I find that a pupil comprehends a subject very much more easily and readily, if he begins the study of its outlines, such as this volume is intended to be on the History of Education. With this book in the pupil's hands and many of the following list of books in the teacher's hands, and accessible to the pupils, excellent work may be done with the subject.

The books that have been consulted in its composition are Compayre's History of Education, Quick's Educational Reformers, S. G. Williams's History of Education, Painter's History of Education, Browning's Educational Theories, Boone's Education in the United States, Schepmoes's Rise and Progress of the New York State School System, and others.

THE AUTHOR.

Cooperstown, N. Y., June 1, 1898.

NOTE TO THE SECOND EDITION.

The edition that was published last year was received with so much favor that the author has been encouraged to rewrite the book. This revision has two to three times as much matter in it as the first edition had. In its present form it is free from errors that are incident to first editions, and contains such changes as are necessary to keep the book abreast with the times.

THE AUTHOR.

Cooperstown, N. Y., July 18, 1899.

...The History of Education...

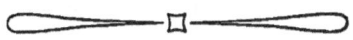

CHAPTER I.

CHINESE.

China is one of the oldest nations of the world, but the Chinese civilization of to-day is practically what it was centuries ago. They are not progressive in government and certainly not in education. Their education is formal, mechanical and traditional. No innovations are tolerated. Mental development is not sought after; memory of past usages is a result.

Children are sent to school at six or seven years of age and taught to read and write. This is a difficult accomplishment, because the Chinese language is one of sign-characters. Morality is taught and honor to parents inculcated. Punishments are severe. Examinations in school and those to secure political preferment are required and difficult.

Results: People patient, outwardly moral, hypocritical and in authority tyrannical, no hope of a life beyond the grave, parents honored by children, persons in authority respected, memory trained, education ancestral.

The greatest educator that China ever had was Confucius, who died in 478 B. C. The date of his birth is uncertain. His renown has given his descendants the highest honors to be bestowed by the empire. His writings have been, from his time to the present, the principal objects of study in all the schools of the empire. The scope of his philosophy is limited to the present life; his sayings do not indicate that he had any definite belief in an existence after death. His precepts are noted for their practical wisdom. He did what he could to give efficacy to the thought that lies as the basis of the Chinese government—the ruler should be as a father and the people as children. His sayings, found in the "Analects," indicate his genius and character. Some of these are— Learning without thought is labor lost. The necessary conditions of government are sufficiency of food, military equipment and confidence of the people in their ruler. What you do not like when done to yourself, do not do to others.

HINDOOS.

The Hindoos live in India and are a branch of the Aryan race. The wealth of their country has led different European countries to seek its conquest. It is now under the control of England and its ancient laws and customs are rapidly becoming things of the past.

Their education is a caste system. The child at six or seven is sent to school, which is presided over by a Brahman, who receives no salary. Gifts from his patrons are his only means of remuneration. He is held in great reverence. Reading, writing, ceremonial customs, morality, and arithmetic are taught. Women are not educated. A twelve year course was provided for after the elementary course was taken. This course was chiefly intended for the Brahmans, though students for the second and third castes might take it. It embraced grammar, history, philosophy, mathematics, law, medicine, astronomy and poetry. The Hindoos made great proficiency in astronomy and mathematics. They are supposed to have originated the decimal system of notation.

Brahmanism is the religion of the people and the Brahmans are the educated persons. Sanskrit is the language of the people and the Veda is one of the principal books in it. The people believe that God is in everything, hence all things in nature are divine.

There are four classes of society: 1st, Brahmans, or holy teachers; 2d, kings and soldiers; 3d, traders; 4th, servants. Social standing and vocation are determined by the accident of birth. Personal talent and individuality are therefore crushed out. This could lead to nothing else than a voluntary abasement and a contempt for the high aspirations of life.

The caste system has made the Hindoos "contented with their lot—whether good or bad, high or low—and in doing so has provided a kind of universal happiness, which, if not of the highest kind, was better than none." They lack force of character to lift them to a high degree of civilization.

ISRAELITES.

A study of the theocratic education of the Jews is very interesting. They were surrounded by idolatrous peoples but were steadfast in their worship of the true God. The character of the civilization of Europe and America can be traced to the Jews.

The child at six entered school. Boys learned reading,

writing, natural history, astronomy, and geometry. The Bible was early used. Girls learned to prepare the food for the table, to make cloth, and to sing and dance. Great stress was put upon moral and religious instruction and love of country. The father was the principal teacher. "Family life is the origin of the primitive society where the notion of the state is almost unknown, and where God is the real king." The child was taught to be the faithful servant of God. A love of country, and a knowledge of the Jews' past history were inculcated at the three annual festivals, the passover, the pentecost and the feast of the tabernacles. The celebration of these festivals compelled every adult to appear annually before the temple in Jerusalem. Great reverence was shown teachers. In dicipline the Jews believed, "He that spareth his rod, hateth his son, but he that loveth him chasteneth him betimes."

The ideal sought after in education was the perfect man. "Ye shall be holy, for I the Lord your God am holy!" "Therefore shall ye lay up these my words in your heart and in your soul, and bind them for a sign upon your hand, that they may be as frontlets between your eyes. * * * And thou shall write them upon the door-posts of thine house and upon the gates." It would appear from this that the ability to read and write was compulsory. Besides the schools conducted by the parents, there were the schools of the prophets, presided over by venerable and able men. These were for the study of medicine, poetry and law.

Before the advent of Christianity, education was domestic; after its introduction, it became public. In 64 A. D. each town was compelled to support a public school. The Jews had a contempt for other people and their education. There were a few Jewish scholars, however, who read Plato and Aristotle.

EGYPTIANS.

The pyramids and other remains of Egypt's past glory indicate that the Egyptians were a wise and intelligent people. They were probably the first civilized people in the world. Philosophers from other countries came here to learn of the wisdom of a people who furnished a Moses and a Solomon. They had a knowledge of many arts, unknown to-day. The colored decorations found in their ruined temples have not been reproduced since their time. They manufactured glass, were skilled at spinning and weaving, and were expert in iron and steel manufacturing.

Their system of education was priestly. The people were divided into castes, the priests occupying the highest one. The priests had fabulous wealth, exercised a wide influence, and had the best education that any land could afford. The priesthood was strictly hereditary. The priests were well versed in all knowledge of their day, since out of their numbers came the physicians, judges. civil officers and councilors of the king, who also was of them. After the priestly class, came in order the military class, the farmers, the mechanics, and the common laborers.

The education of the lower classes, which was under the management of the priests, was elementary. The tradesmen were taught reading, writing and arithmetic, the latter concretely by plays. The others were taught by their parents to do what the accident of birth destined them to do. Writing was largely hieroglyphic. Paper was made from the papyrus plant. The lower classes were taught to reverence the priesthood, religion and traditional customs.

Among the noted institutions for the education of the priests were those at Thebes and Memphis. Music and gymnastics were not considered means of culture. Greek was not taught until the seventh century B. C.

PHOENICIANS.

Phoenicia extends along the eastern coast of the Mediterranean through about two degrees of latitude. Some believe that the Phoenicians were a distinct race from the Hebrews, others that they were an offshoot from the Semitic stock. The Phoenician dialect was closely akin to Hebrew. Their religion was pantheistic. The rivers were sacred to gods and the trees to goddesses.

Their education was largely commercial. Their maritime enterprise excelled that of any other nation of antiquity. The young were taught such subjects as would make them expert navigators and expert commercial people.

To them is ascribed the invention of arithmetic, of our alphabet, and of writing. Next after the Jews, they have exerted the widest influence upon the Western world.

CHAPTER II.

EDUCATION AMONG THE GREEKS.

Greece is about the size of Maine. It is the oldest civilized country in Europe. Its climate is healthful, its soil rich, its hills and valleys picturesque, and its coasts deeply indented. It is adapted to be the home of a progressive and cultured people. Anciently, Greece was divided into a number of small states. Athens and Sparta, cities in two of these states, had noted systems of education and illustrious educators.

The ancient Greeks attained a higher degree of intellectual activity than had existed up to their time. Their downfall at the hands of the conquering Romans checked the cause of education, and not until the revival of learning in the 15th century did Europe rise to the intellectual level of ancient Greece. The Greeks were eminent in philosophy, literature, geography, the fine arts, mathematics, and oratory. The study that students of the last few centuries have given to these branches of Greek learning has contributed not a little to modern culture.

From Homer, we learn that respect for parents, silence in the presence of elders, modesty, and chastity were characteristics in the training of the young. Obedience in youth was inculcated that the citizen might the better know how to command. The father taught his son the use of arms, how to properly exercise his body, and the worship of the gods; the mother taught her daughter prudence and virtue. The high ideals held up to the admiration of the young Grecian student had much to do in forming in him high aspirations and noble impulses. A noble view was taken of the state. Education was a favorite topic of legislative discussion and many wise laws were passed regarding it. The interest of the state seems to have been paramount; the interest of the individual of a secondary nature.

There were several schools of philosophy in Greece that had a great influence upon the destinies of her people and upon those of other nations where these schools were transferred. Chief among these schools were the Epicureans, founded by Epicurus about 300 B. C., and the Stoics, founded by Zeno at about the same time. Epicurus taught "a happy life, a quiet and cheerful mind, and an undisturbed enjoyment of pleasure as the highest attainable good.—Intellectual pleasures were valued by him more highly than sensual ones, and friendship, tranquility, patience and suffering unavoidable pain." Epicurus and his immediate followers led pure lives, but his doctrine in the hands of the Romans led to licentiousness and is considered by some to be one of the causes of the downfall of their empire. The Stoics laid great stress upon "the control of passions and emotions, upon the subordination of the body to the mind, upon refraining from sensual pleasures and upon every kind of abstinence and self-denial. Even life itself should be relinquished, if it hindered the exercise of conscience. Stoicism was the symbol of austere morality."

With the downfall of Greece, Greek culture was transferred to Alexandria, Egypt. Here Neoplatonism, the effort "to harmonize oriental theology with Greek dialectics," flourished. Here was formed the first school for the study of Christian theology.

The new Testament and the early literature of the church were written in Greek. This will always give the study of Greek a place in our schools.

About 300 A.D., Constantine made Constantinople the capital of the Roman empire, where Greek literature prevailed. Theodosius, a little later divided the empire into two parts. The Eastern empire was largely Greek in civilization. It had a miserable existence until it was captured by the Turks. The Turks were opposed to the Greek religion. Most of the Greek scholars had to leave for other countries. The opposition of the Turks to Greek learning continued down to the eighteenth century, when the Turks felt that their authority was firmly established.

ATHENS.

The Athenian education has been called aesthetic. Children were taught to read and swim. The state saw that the children attended the gymnasium while the private individual organized schools for music and grammar. Later Athens required a literary training. The Athenian child was kept in charge of a nurse until he was six or seven, when he was put in charge of a pedagogue, who was usually a slave, and who was more an attendant than a teacher. If the child was not kept in school by his parents, he was not compelled to support them in their old age. The elementary schools had two teachers—the grammatist who taught the child reading and writing, and the critic, who explained the poets to him and and heard him recite from them. He attended successively the school for grammar, the palestra (a gymnastic school), and the school for music. This took eighteen years. The wax tablet and the stylus were the writing materials. The Iliad and the Odyssey were among the first books used. Passages from these were committed.

At fourteen the poor children learned a trade and the wealthy took up grammar, music, rhetoric, poetry, mathematics and philosophy. In the elementary gymnastic schools, running, jumping, wrestling and similar sports were taught. Mental culture was sought after with this training. Later the state gymnasia gave this physical exercise a more manly character. By means of this training, the Athenians sought after beauty of body, while the Spartans sought after strength and endurance.

The education of any Grecian that lacked music was regarded defective. The laws of Greece were set to music. The Grecians argued that music inspired the soul and soothed the passions. It softened the manners of those men who otherwise would have been fierce through their physical training.

Discipline was severe. Aristophanes says, "The boys came out of each street with bare heads and feet, and, regardless of rain or snow, went together in the most perfect order towards the school of music. They were seated quietly and modestly. They were not permitted to cross their legs. * * * If some one took a notion to sing with soft and studied inflections, he was severely flogged."

At eighteen the youth entered the military system of the state. Two years later he became a voter and received the privileges of a citizen.

The moral standard of the Greeks was not high. The Greek could not rise above his gods. These were deified beings, beautiful in body, but fillèd with base passions. The moral and useful were of more significance than was the beautiful. The slaves were not educated and the women were in servile subordination. "Patriotism and courage, respect for religious rites of the city, modesty and urbanity of manner, a constant regard for outward propriety, were carefully inculcated. The refined taste of the Athenian abolished grossness from his vices."

SPARTA.

The Spartan education is known as martial education and was devised by Lycurgus, the law-giver of Sparta. It fostered a contempt for life and worldly goods, but the habit of prompt obedience to all the demands of the state. It abated pride and luxury, and led to simplicity of living. The interests of the state were regarded superior to those of the individual, therefore the child was regarded as the property of the state. Unhealthy children were allowed to be killed.

Up to the seventh year the mother used all known resources to invigorate her child's body. After this they were taken from their homes and placed under the most severe discipline. Their food was coarse; their clothing scanty; and their bed was made of rushes. Their bodies were bathed on certain days of the year only and therefore became hard and dry. Thieving was permitted. The thief became very adroit in concealing his theft. He was severely whipped if detected. Reading and writing were taught, but not so thoroughly as in Athens. The youth associated with the old, from whom they obtained lessons of practical wisdom. Through the same source, they learned about state affairs, how to behave mannerly and to acquire a dignified bearing. Drunkenness was little known in Sparta. The Spartan youth was temperate in habit, respectful to his elders, and obedient to parents. He revered past usages, was inured to cold and hunger, and ready to die for his country. The mother was content if her son died facing the enemy. Spartan women received training in the gymnasium, and became noted for their strength and beauty.

The Spartan education "aimed at training men who were to live in the midst of difficulty and danger, and could be safe themselves only while they held rule over others. The citizen was to be equally fitted to command and to obey. The Spartan system attained, within its own sphere, to a perfection which it is impossible not to admire."

COMPARISON OF ATHENIAN AND SPARTAN EDUCATION.

"At Athens, while not neglecting the body, the chief preoccupation is the training of the mind; intellectual culture is pushed to an extreme, even to over refinement; there is such a taste for fine speaking that it develops an abuse of language and reasoning which merits the disreputable name of sophistry. At Sparta, the mind is sacrificed to body; physical strength and military skill are the qualities most desired; the sole care is the training of athletes and soldiers. Sobriety and courage are the results of this one-sided education, but so are ignorance and brutality."

At Sparta, "the education was cruel, with but a trace

of the intellectual. Mercy, tenderness, sympathy, the poetry of life, were, if known, despised. * * * *
The Athenian education emphasized the duty of every citizen to the state—but only that the state might better enable those citizens to enjoy prosperity and the fruits of an honorable peace. Athens could fight bravely, but she did not, like Sparta, crave for war. Strength she sought, but with grace and above all wisdom. Woman was wife, as well as mother, and the family was the guardian of the child."

EFFECT OF GREEK EDUCATION ON MODERN EDUCATION.

The effect of Greek education on modern education is variously estimated by students of history. It is certain that modern education owes much to the ancient Greeks. We have received from them, grammar, rhetoric, logic, ethics, economics, geometry, drawing, mechanics and the fine arts. They have contributed to our notion of beauty, culture, harmony and grace.

CHAPTER III.

GRECIAN EDUCATION

SOCRATES. (469-399 B. C.)

Socrates' father was a sculptor. Socrates was a man inferior in personal appearance and not graceful in bearing, but full of noble thoughts and aspirations. He was strong and courageous. He left no writings, but his mode of teaching, the Socratic, has been retained to the present time.

He taught in the streets of Athens and in other public places. He is the author of the developing method. By a series of questions, he showed his pupils the soundness or unsoundness of their opinions and excited in them the utmost mental activity. Truth was always the object of his inquiries.

The Sophists, who lived at his time, were the direct product of the Athenian education. They were clever in argument, but had little reverence for religion. They prided themselves upon being able to argue ingeniously in favor of whatever they wished. Socrates believed in one Supreme God. It was for him to show the Sophists the evils of their ways. For this he lost his life.

When an error was made in reply to a question, Socrates oftentimes seemed to accept it as a truth, but by skilfully questioning his student, he would show the error in its true light. This is known as Socratic irony. The Socratic method, called maieutics, is the art of giving birth to ideas.

Socrates' maxim was, "Know thyself." He looked upon self knowledge as the only true sense of wisdom. He believed that if man would learn the truth, he would be impelled to thought and action. To assist men after true wisdom was the purpose of his teaching.

The process of his method is of great educational value. He has shown us how to apply it. He always proceeded from the known to the unknown; from the easy to the difficult. He explained by way of comparison or analogy. The immediate product of his method is clearness of conception. The result of his teaching led to a reconstruction of fundamental ideas in many departments of inquiry. Sophistry was dissipated by his questioning.

He "believed teaching to be a divine calling. The teacher should be an adept in the art of teaching. This was, in his opinion, of greater worth than material knowledge. He should be a man of mature age and intellectual force, whose sympathy for his pupils is deep and powerful and will never forsake them. He should understand the art of developing ideas from within the mind of the pupil, by arousing his mind to self activity through skilful questioning."

Xenophon says of him: "He was so pious that he did nothing without the advice of the gods; so just that he never in the least injured anyone; so fully master of himself that he never chose the pleasant instead of the good; so discriminating that he never failed to distinguish the better from the worse."

But this pure man was not understood by the corrupted populace of Athens and he was accused of corrupting the Athenian youth and decrying the gods recognized by the state. He was condemned to death and perished in the seventy-first year of his age.

PLATO. (429-347 B. C.)

Plato claims among his ancestors Codrus and Solon, the law-giver of Athens. There is a fable that bees settled on his lips in infancy. He was a great traveler and observer. His writings show that he was familiar with the noted Greek writings of his day. He was one of Socrates' most distinguished pupils. He was melancholy and thoughtful. He rarely smiled and never laughed. He is the first to subject education to a scientific examination.

After studying in Syracuse and elsewhere, he returned to Athens where he established a school of philosophy, called the Academy. The school was established in a small garden, adorned with statues, temples, surrounded with beautiful trees, and intersected by a winding stream. Here he promulgated his theories of idealism. Ideas, according to him, are the eternal types, constituting the essence of things. "These ideas are the substance of all knowledge, and the human intellect attains to the knowledge of them by dialectics, that is, systematic examination and argument, by which the non-essential are distinguished from the essential elements." The school of Plato was a university training; it made its students philosophers, when it would have been better for the state to have introduced men to public and practical life. His training did much for science; it did a great service for geometry especially.

Republic is the title of his chief work on education. In this he argues that "the state is but the citizen writ large." Education should be under the control of the state. Children should be kept with their parents until they are seven, and be taught morality by myths. He considers honor to parents, love of fellow-citizens, self-control, truthfulness and courage to be cardinal virtues, and the stability of the state to depend upon a correct knowledge of music. He advocates athletics and dialectics. At twenty men are to be selected for their employments. For the following ten years, they are to study science, as applied to war; then for the following five, they are to study dialectics. Dialectics, according to Plato, enables one to "fight his way as it were, through all objections, studying to disprove them, not by rules of opinion, but by those real existence * * * without making one false step in his train of thought." This study is to be followed by fifteen years of public service. Plato says, "Education is nurture. It can determine whether a nature shall be wild and malevolent or rich with benefits to mankind. It includes not merely instruction or training, but all the influences that are brought to bear on the soul. The soul is made up of three parts: 1, the appetite, which is wild but capable of being tamed; 2, the spirit, the element of courage; 3, the philosophic element, the source of gentleness, of love, of culture." In the elaborate system of education, Plato omits the physical and natural sciences, because, "in his mystic idealism, things of sense are delusive and unreal images, and so did not appear to him worthy of arresting the attention of the mind."

His Laws was the work of his mature years. It qualifies many of the propositions found in the Republic. It is far more practical and less radical than his former work. In it, he says, "A good education is that which gives to the body and to the soul all the beauty and all the perfection of which they are capable *   *   *
A free mind ought to learn nothing as a slave. The lesson that is made to enter the mind by force will not remain there. Then use no violence toward children; the rather, cause them to learn while playing. *   *   *
I am persuaded that the inclination to humor the likings of children is the surest of all ways to spoil them. We should not make too much haste in our search after what is pleasurable, especially as we shall never be wholly exempt from what is painful." Plato in all his works seems to have made a "constant search for a higher morality."

ARISTOTLE. (429-347 B. C.)

Aristotle was Plato's most famous pupil and the teacher of Alexander the Great. He is known as "the Alexander of the intellectual world." Plato said of him that he was "the intellect of his school." He reduced geometry to a science, originated the study of natural history and invented logic.

The philosophy of Aristotle is more practical than Plato's. Aristotle's investigations were the result of painstaking research; they were not theoretical. He knew the pleasures of family association and had trained his own children. These experiences made him a competent educator. Plato was an idealist; Aristotle was a realist, and the father of experimental science. His method of teaching was analytic. His philosophy was based on the principle that all knowledge is founded on the observation of facts. Pedagogy must be based on principles derived from the knowledge of men. Happiness is the goal of activity and is acquired by performing moral action. The state should establish the happiness of families and communities. The same education does not produce the same effect in all individuals, because character is dependent upon nature, habit and instruction.

At fifty he founded in Athens the Lyceum. He walked with his pupils through the shady grove, where the school was held, while teaching; this has given the name peripatetic to his school of philosophy. He gave lectures mornings and afternoons. Those of the afternoons were less abstruse than those of the morning. "His principal object is to examine truth under all her aspects, never to stop beyond the probable and to bring his philosophical system in unison with the general opinion of men as suggested by common sense, observation and experience."

He believed in public education, but that parents should not relinquish their care over their children as the Spartans did. He argues that courses of discipline should bring out in their proper relation the physical, the moral and the intellectual parts of the child. Among the elements of instruction, he includes grammar, gymnastics, music and drawing.

His principal work is Politics. This contains theory of instruction, and is not so valuable to a student of pedagogy as are his lectures in the Lyceum. In it he says that a good education has four branches—gymnastics, music, grammar and the art of designs.

The pedagogy of Aristotle was for the few. His system of education was for the free-born. Slaves and women were practically excluded from it. The studies that he recommended were of the intellectual type; they were not utilitarian. The Greek systems of education were not adapted to a Christian civilization.

"Plato attaches great importance to mathematics, because it leads from the concrete to the abstract, from the real to the ideal. Aristotle assigns a subordinate place to it because it has no bearing upon the ethical nature of man. Plato opposes poets and artists, whom Aristotle commends; Plato sought religion in ceremonies Aristotle found it in the heart of man."

"Aristotle is the connecting link between Greek civilization and the European civilization of later periods; through him and because of him Greek civilization expanded into European civilization, and into the cosmopolitan civilization of our days—the civilization that asks not after nationality, or birth, or station or sex, but that would unite all human beings in the great brother- and sisterhood of strong individuals, whose equal privilege is happiness."

XENOPHON. (444-354 B. C.)

Xenophon was one of the most illustrious scholars of Socrates. He is chiefly noted for writing Economics, Cyropoedia and Anabasis. The Economics was written under the influence of his famous teacher, and gives a scheme for the education of woman. Before Xenophon's time, the Athenian woman's virtues were purely negative. He "assigns to her husband the duty of training her mind and of teaching her the positive duties of family life,—order, economy, kindness to slaves, and tender care of children." In the Cyropoedia, he describes the Persian education and a plan of an education uniform and military. He cites incidents in the life of Cyrus to show the justice of Persian education. But it is easy to show that the Persian education was one-sided. The intellectual part of man was not developed; the physical and the moral were, because their development was useful in war and in the administration of justice. The Anabasis contains a true account of the Persian government at that time. It had a great influence upon Alexander the Great. It was the first work of its kind in Greece.

EUCLID.

Probably Euclid lived during the reign of Ptolemy I. (323-285 B. C.) He undoubtedly founded the mathematical school of Alexandria. But little is known of his life. The man must be studied through his written works. The greatest of these is his Elements of Geometry, in thirteen books, known as Euclid. The extent of his treatise would indicate that he spoke correctly when he said "There is no royal road to geometry." For an analysis of the Euclid, the student is referred to the Encyclopedia Britannica. His Elements of Geometry is the most ancient system that is extant, and has been considered standard for 2,000 years.

STRABO. (54 ? B. C.—-24 ? A. D.)

Strabo was born at Amasia in Pontus. He received a good education in the Greek poets. He studied at

Athens, Rome and Alexandria. His travels extended to many cities and through many countries.

The first attempt, so far as known, to gather all attainable geographical knowledge in a general treatise on Geography was made by Strabo. His Geography, in seventeen books, was intended to be a sequel to his historical materials, obtained through his extended travels. The work was intended for the statesman rather than the student. It gives valuable information on ethnology, trade and metallurgy.

PTOLEMY. (SECOND CENTURY A. D.)

Ptolemy was a native of Egypt, but the date and place of birth and the date of his death are uncertain or unknown. He is noted as a mathematician, astronomer and geographer. The Almagest contains his mathematical researches and greatly influenced the students of astronomy. One of the results of his astronomical investigations is the famous Ptolemaic system of planetary motion. Through his investigations in trigonometry, astronomy attained its final general construction. His work on Geography was the first to place the subject on a scientific basis.

PYTHAGORAS. (580 B. C —-).

Pythagoras was born on Samos, but was allied in spirit to the Spartans. He left no written records, hence many mythical stories are told about him. His travels in Egypt greatly influenced his teaching. He founded a famous school at Crotona, in southern Italy. The course was divided into two parts. It was during the second part that the student came into close relations with the great master. The students were taught mathematics, music, medicine, physics, geography, and metaphysics. He was especially fond of mathematics and discovered that the square of the hypothenuse of a right triangle is equivalent to the squares of its two legs. His instruction was dogmatic. Assertions made by Pythagoras were regarded true because he made them. His system was "strict in morals, severe in discipline, partial to physical training, authoritative in method, and aristocratic in tendency." It was on account of its aristocratic tendencies that the Crotona school was attacked by a mob and burned. Pythagoras was not heard of after this.

His method of instruction showed Spartan influence, in strictness in morals, in the importance given to gymnastics, in its positive methods, in the scanty diet to which he subjected his pupils, and in its aristocratic tendencies.

The cardinal principle of his system was metempsychosis, or the transmigration of the soul. He tried to introduce into the human soul the harmony which he observed in the universe. "Self-knowledge he regarded as the indispensable condition for self-improvement—as the basis of all culture, the highest aim of which is to obtain a full understanding of the essence and relations of the objects around us, and to live in harmony with them. Music was in itself one of the most important instruments of this culture, embodying and typifying the harmony of the universe, as well as aiding the soul in its efforts to bring itself into the same harmony." It may be seen that harmony was the chief thing sought after in his system of education.

He taught slowly what he attempted to teach; his pupils therefore assimilated what they were instructed in. But he did not appreciate the inaccuracies of the scientific statements of his time and taught many hypotheses as truths. His students became arrogant and prided themselves as being superior to other persons. This aroused the hatred of these persons, and was a cause of the overthrow of the school at Crotona.

CHAPTER IV.

ROMAN EDUCATION.

In the Roman education the family occupied the highest place. The Roman mother had the exclusive care of her child during its early years. After slavery had spread over the empire, the mother gave way to the corrupt influences of that system and placed her child into the hands of nurses. Then it was that only the poorest mothers took care of their children. In the palmiest days of Rome, the Roman matron attended to the physical wants of her children, to their moral sentiments, their language, and their religious feelings. The father was the master of the family and could even take the life of his own child. He supplemented the labors of the mother in the matter of instruction. He saw that his boys were familiar with the gods of the family and of the state, with the laws of the government, with military and civil instruction and that they were prepared for a trade. The Romans had no idea of education by the state; the children were taught at home.

At seven the child was taught the elements of reading and writing by the literator. Reading was taught by explaining the power of the letters in combination before their individual characteristics, i. e., by the syllabic method. Writing was taught by the pupil tracing with a stylus letters inscribed on a waxen tablet. Words were then pronounced with their proper accent. Poets were read and selections memorized. Reckoning followed. The fingers and joints of the hand were used for this purpose. At twelve the child was placed in the hands of the literatus for more advanced work. Greek was added to Latin. Morality was taught through explanations of the poets. History, especially that relating to the laws of the land, was carefully studied. Oratory received early attention. At fifteen, the youth assumed the dress of manhood and chose his profession. The Roman mother had a strong influence over her children. She stimulated her sons to great effort in war and in the forum. The Roman boy sat at the table with his father and listened, in silence, to the recital of what his ancestors had done for his country, and often accompanied him to the Senate to learn how to act on public occasions. The rod was not spared. The ability to read and write was a rare accomplishment. The children of the rich were instructed, but those of the poor could not afford an education. The early history of Rome was transmitted by oral instruction, for writing was but little practiced before the Greeks were conquered.

THE GRECIAN AND THE ROMAN EDUCATION COMPARED.

The Grecian education produced men "beautiful, active, clever, receptive, emotional, quick to feel and show his feeling, to argue, to refine; greedy of the pleasures of the world..*..*..*..inquiring into every secret; strongly attached to the things of this life, but elevated by an unabated striving after the highest ideal; setting no value but on faultless abstractions, and seeing reality only in heaven, on earth mere shadows." The Roman education produced men, "practical, energetic, eloquent, tinged but not imbued with philosophy, trained to spare neither himself nor others; reading and thinking only with an apology; best engaged in defending a political principle * * * in leading armies through unexplored deserts, establishing roads, fortresses, settlements, as the result of conquest, or in ordering and superintending the slow, certain and utter annihilation of some enemy of Rome." "In Greece a love for the aesthetic predominated, the Greek taking a peculiar delight in the beautiful; but, with the Roman, the practical prevailed, and the beautiful was simply an aesthetic amusement. He was harder, coarser, delighting more in power and less in beauty, more in facts and less in speculation, more in the real and less in the ideal."

CHAPTER V.

ROMAN EDUCATORS.

QUINTILIAN. (35-95 A. D.)

Quintilian, "professor of eloquence," was born in Spain, but spent his life in Rome. He won distinction at the bar, but early turned his attention to teaching. He was the first teacher in Rome to receive a salary from the state. During his experience of twenty years as a teacher in Rome, he numbered among his pupils some of the foremost men of that city. In his Institutes of Oratory, he gives a treatise on education as well as one on rhetoric.

Intellectual training. according to Quintilian, should begin before the child is seven. It should not be formal, but should be given in the form of plays to develop his intellect. Nurses and mothers should be careful to give the child correct impressions. "Wool, once colored, never regains its primitive whiteness." All children, in normal condition, are teachable. If the promise of youth is not fulfilled, it is attributable to defective education. He used ivory letters to give children the idea of the shape of letters before they were taught their names. He taught everything that he attempted to teach thoroughly, before going to something else. He advocated that instruction should not be reserved until the sixth or seventh year, for memory is tenacious in childhood and it is reasonable to make use of it then. Greek should be taught before Latin, since the Roman child would naturally acquire Latin. The study of Latin should not be too long deferred, lest a pure pronunciation be lost.

Public education had a zealous and intelligent advocate in Quintilian. The pupil does not receive more care from a single teacher. The best teachers, with all that implies, will be found in the large schools. Vices are not taught children in school, but the children bring them there. Common sense cannot be effectively taught in a private school. The public school brings its pupils in contact with each other. Ambition is excited by seeing the advancement made by associates. Quintilian says, "We form the palate of our children before we form their pronunciation. They grow up in the sedan chairs; if they touch the ground, they hang by the hands of attendants supporting them on each side. We are delighted if they utter anything immodest. * * * Need we be astonished at their behavior? We have taught them." He argues that the public school tends to rectify this condition.

It was Quintilian's plan to make lawyers and statesmen. The public school was necessary to accomplish this. The orator, who must be active in public affairs, must accustom himself from boyhood to the society and activity of man. His Institutes of Oratory gives in detail the essentials necessary to an orator. He must be a good man, must be well versed in logic, ethics, and physics, and so forth.

Corporal punishment should not be allowed, because it is servile and degrading; after a time it loses its effect, and if steady work be given, there will be no occasion for it.

PLUTARCH. (50 to 138 A. D.)

Plutarch was born in Chaeronea, but early went to Rome. He did not attach himself to any school of Philosophy, but was an independent thinker. He was conversant with history and physics. He applied his learning to the casualties of human existence. He held that the soul is imperishable. He is particularly famous for his "Forty-six Parallel Lives." The author sets a Greek warrior, statesman, orator, or legislator side by side with noted Romans celebrated for the same qualities. Nearly all the lives are in pairs, but the work concludes with a few single biographies. His treatment is not always impartial; he sympathizes too much with the Spartan character to be free from impartiality. Plutarch says in his "Opera Moralia," "Kindness and advice better than blows; over-pressure in learning is to be avoided; gradual advance in virtue is like steady sailing over a wide sea, and can only be measured by the time taken and the force applied."

In his treatise On the Education of Children, he says that the aim of education is the virtuous man, that education depends on natural gifts, training, and exercise, and that teachers of boys should have experience and have a blameless character. Gymnastic exercise is necessary to a good education; scolding is needless and self-control is to be learned.

Plutarch writes only in behalf of the free-born. He believes that the state should not usurp the function of the family in the training of children. Contrary to Quintilian, he believes that the state does not exercise absolute sovereignty in society. He recommends an education that is domestic. That this kind of training may be perfected, he exalts the condition of woman, who should instruct her offspring. Plutarch gave the world the first formal treatise on the education of children.

PLINY. (23-79 A. D.)

Pliny, the naturalist, was a great student, and a temperate and clear thinker. No Roman gained more renown as an investigator of the phenomena of nature than he. He had a great influence on the nomenclature and the popular ideas about common objects. His diligence was proverbial. While riding or being carried in a litter, he continued his studies. He had a slave read to him while at his meals. His zeal for investigation cost him his life. He ventured too near Vesuvius at the destruction of Pompeii to get a good view of the mountain and was suffocated by the sulphurous vapors.

His greatest work is Natural History, in thirty-seven volumes. It is well preserved to-day. It contains facts on botany, zoology, astronomy, the arts, etc. It was the Roman Encyclopaedia. The work is largely a compilation. Pantheistic ideas run through it. With all its faults it is an astounding movement of industry.

VARRO. (116-26 B. C.)

Varro, "the most learned man in Rome," was the first Roman beyond the Alps to win eminence in literature. He lived in the turbulent times of Marius and Sulla and had all of his immense wealth confiscated. He sought relief from these harassing circumstances in literature. He began the study of Greek at thirty-five. Caesar made him librarian. He is said to have written 620 books on 74 different topics. He wrote on grammar, history, rhetoric, and geometry. These were instrumental in the education of several generations. His most valuable work was on agriculture, a hand-book for the Italian farmer. His writings show spirit and vigor.

SENECA. (2 B. C. ?-65 A. D.)

Seneca was born at Cordova, Spain, but early went to Rome, where he spent his life. After traveling in Greece and Egypt, he returned to Rome and practiced law. During his banishment for eight years to Corsica, he studied philosophy. He expressed a rational contempt for the instruction imparted to him in his youth. He became the tutor to Nero. He could not control the depravity of that profligate emperor. He was condemned to death in 65 A. D.

His Letters to Lucilius contains some pedagogical precepts. He "criticises confused and ill-directed reading that does not enrich the understanding and recommends the profound study of a single book." He says, "The best means for giving clearness to one's own ideas is to communicate them to others; the best way of being taught is to teach; the end is attained sooner by example than by precept."

Seeing the corruption of his own age, Seneca advocated the education of growth in pure morals, self-control and truthfulness, and that God can inspire every man, though by nature corrupt, with upright and pure thoughts. He saw that a teacher must be versatile, since children possess a variety of individualities. He advocated practical and useful studies. "Non scholae, sed vitae discimus."

ST. JEROME. (330 ?—420 A.D.)

St. Jerome was born at Stridon. His parents were Christians and wealthy. He completed his education at Rome. In the Roman schools of philosophy he listened to lectures on Plato and other Greek philosophers. His Sundays were spent in the catacombs deciphering inscriptions on the graves of the martyrs. He was a man of strong opinions and sacrificed friends for them. During a severe illness he became converted to Christianity, and his conversion was so pronounced that he resolved to renounce whatever kept him from God. He loved to study the literature of pagan Rome. In his dreams, God reproached him with caring more to be a Ciceronian than a Christian. He taught the beauties of monastic life, and probably the first to teach physical asceticism; that is, the body is an enemy that must be subdued by abstinence and by mortifications of the flesh. Paula a wealthy Roman lady, impressed with his teaching, built four monasteries, three for nuns and one for monks, over one of which she placed Jerome.

His translation of the Scriptures in Latin is known as the vulgate, and is the one used in the Roman Catholic church to-day.

His letters on the education of girls forms the most valuable educational document written during the fourth century.

ST. AUGUSTINE. (354-430 A. D.)

St. Augustine was born in Numidia and educated at Carthage. His father was a pagan; his mother a zealous Christian. He was well educated in the best schools of Carthage and elsewhere. The fascination of the Carthaginian theatres drew him from Christianity, but he never forgot the pious teaching of his mother. He changed from one religious faith to another until he came under the influence of St. Ambrose, who, with the entreaties of his mother, converted him to the Christian faith. He became the most influential writer and advocate of that doctrine that the world had had.

His works form a library. The most noted of these are his Confessions and his City of God, one of the most remarkable productions of all Christian writings. His Confessions, as the title indicates, narrates the struggles in his soul which resulted in his conversion. The City of God answers the charge of the pagans that Christianity was the cause of the calamities which befell Rome. He shows in the Confessions the influence of maternal education upon the life of man, and the effect of the intellectual aspirations of man and his moral nature. He opposed the reading by the young of the "impious fables of poets, the published lies of the rhetoricians, and the verbose subtleties of the philosophers." The use of pagan classics in Christian schools is questioned to-day. He advocated special training for candidates for the priesthood. He was the father of Christian catechetics.

CHAPTER VI.

EFFECT OF CHRISTIANITY ON EDUCATION.

Pagan education was one-sided; it did not give a complete development to man's character. The advent of Christ was destined to change character. Christianity teaches the brotherhood of mankind, and that God is no respecter of persons. It seeks to overthrow the injustice of society. It gives woman an honorable position by the side of man. "Christianity taught that man no longer belonged to society except in part; that he was under allegiance to it by his body and his material interests; that being subject to a tyrant, he must submit; he ought to give his life for it; but that in respect of his soul, he was free, and owed allegiance only to God." Thus, Christianity does away the distinctions of class and caste and the notion that the state is superior to the individual.

Christian education up to the Reformation met with strong opposition. Its efficiency was crippled by being brought in contact with existing customs and by being united with the State. A corrupt priesthood tainted it with tyranny. But during those years of tyranny and superstition, the relics of ancient literature were preserved in the monasteries, and popular education had a beginning.

Though there was self-sacrificing devotion manifested during those years, educational training was incomplete among primitive Christians. It subordinated the intellectual and even the physical to the moral and religious elements of our nature.

There was a poverty of educational thought during the first centuries. The barbarous people among whom the early Christians worked could not rise to a high mental culture. These centuries were full of conquest and wars which left but little opportunity for educational study. The early Christians sought to annihilate existing beliefs; they could not suddenly expect to receive the sympathy of those whom they endeavored to instruct in an opposing faith.

At the close of the second century, the regenerating influence of Christianity began to show itself upon the poor and lowly. "The lovely character of Christian women was viewed with amazement by their heathen neighbors." The first Christian school of high grade was located at Alexandria in 181 A. D.. Kingsley's "Hypatia" shows the condition of this period quite faithfully.

During the fourth and fifth centuries, the power of Rome tried to crush out the growing influence of Christian teaching. The high morality of the persecuted won, however, the respect of the pagan writers. The Emperor Constantine became converted to the new faith. This support of the empire produced for it rapid growth. But the barbarian invasions of the next two centuries checked its spreading influence. The principal teaching was the doctrines of the church. The learning of the preceding centuries was in the Latin language and it had so much paganism in it that the church did not teach it, since the mind was regarded of less value than the soul. Alcuin, St. Augustine and many other writers of the time were convinced that

"Christianity was alien to Roman culture." Symonds says, "The adoption of intellectual interest in theological questions, contributed to destroy what remained of sound scholarship in the last years of the empire."

Christianity during the fifteenth century desired to win people to a better life. The Italian renaissance of this time desired "to acquire and to transmit to Europe a knowledge of the classics." Symonds again says, "The culture of the classics had to be reappropriated before the movement of the modern mind could begin. This task was effected by long and toilsome study, by the accumulation of manuscripts, by the acquisition of dead languages, by the solitary labors of grammarians, by the lectures of itinerant professors, by the scribe, by the printing-press, by the self-devotion of magnificent Italy to erudition."

CHAPTER VII.

EDUCATION DURING MIDDLE AGES.

A peculiar tendency of the education of the Church during the middle ages was asceticism, or a disdain of this life in the interest of the life to come. Since the people thought that the body was the seat of sin, it was restrained and often scourged that the soul might attain thereby a greater perfection. The hermits, who withdrew from society, and the monks, who lived in poverty and under strict physical disipline, were two classes of ascetics.

Worldly interests were largely ignored. The priests exercised great power. They excluded the pagan literature of Greece and Rome from Christian schools. Learning languished. Many of the priests could neither read nor write. Ignorance among men of rank was common. Religion was the chief topic of discussion and thought. Education was fettered for ages. The causes of this state of intellectual darkness up to the revival of learning were, many Christians thought ignorance favored holiness, the barbaric tribes of the North overran Italy and Greece, introducing their rude manners, the social condition of the people was deplorable, and there was a lack of national languages, books and schools.

But the monastic orders of the Benedictines, the Franciscans, and the Dominicans exerted a marked influence for good during these ages. The monasteries of these orders became "asylums for the oppressed; fortresses against violence; missionary stations for the conversion of heathen communities; repositories of learning, homes for the arts and sciences. They preserved and transmitted to later ages much of the learning of antiquity."

The education of the middle ages belongs largely to the age of the Schoolmen. The course of instruction embraced the seven liberal arts, so-called. These were divided into two classes called the trivium, which included Latin grammar, logic and rhetoric, and quadrivium, which included arithmetic, geometry, astronomy and music. Reading and writing were studied under Latin grammar. This course took seven years. This course produced good reasoners but not fully developed men. "Latin, the language of the church, was made the basis of education, to the universal neglect of the mother-tongue."

The relation of the course of study to theology is thus stated by a writer of the ninth century: "Grammar teaches us to understand the old poets and historians and also to speak and write correctly. Rhetoric, which teaches the different kinds and principal parts of discourse, is important only for such youths as have not more serious studies to pursue and should be learned only from the holy fathers. In dialectic or logic, reason dwells and is manifested and developed. Arithmetic is important on account of the secrets contained in its number. Geometry is necessary, because in Scripture circles of all kinds occur in the building of the Ark and Solomon's temple. Music and astronomy are required in connection with divine service."

"The principal effect which the schoolmen had on education was to determine the form in which instruction should be given. They had, at the same time, a considerable indirect influence in stimulating the intellect to speculation, in rousing a dissatisfaction with dogmas which were incapable of proof, and in preparing the way for the reformation."

During the middle ages, there existed the cathedral, parochial schools, and secular schools, which gave knightly education and burgher or town education. The cathedral schools were intended for the instruction of the priesthood. The instruction embraced the seven liberal arts. The parochial schools, supervised by the priest were to teach the young, Christian doctrine, and to prepare them for church-membership. The discipline was very severe.

Knightly education was in sharp contrast with church education. Church education ignored physical training and polished manners. After passing through a vigorous training, a knight took a vow at the age of twenty-one "to speak the truth, defend the right, honor womankind, and use his sword against the infidels of the East." This training led to a love of glory, a beautiful body, polished manners, and a high regard for the honor and virtue of woman.

The burgher schools were the result of the growing power of the trading and artisan classes. Reading, writing and arithmetic were carefully taught. To these subjects were added geography, history, natural science and Latin. The teachers were poorly paid and wandered from place to place in search of employment. They were not well respected.

One product of knightly education was the crusades. They probably, exercised a greater influence to advance civilization during the Middle Ages than any other cause. The crusades were undertaken to rescue the Holy Sepulchre from the infidel Mohammedans. The crusades "enlarged the contracted sphere of human knowledge. Foreign lands, and new customs, science, and arts were introduced into the circle of popular thought. The crusades led to the emancipation of many serfs, and elevated them to the rank of free peasants. They quickened commerce, trade and manufacture; increased and strengthened the burgher class; and extended the power and influence of the cities. The knightly and burgher classes attained to a feeling of self-consciousness and independence. They emancipated themselves, to some extent at least, from ecclesiastical tutelage; and this naturally led to a change in education."

CHAPTER VIII.

MONASTIC SCHOOLS.

Benedictines.—The Benedictines, the Jesuits of the Middle Ages, were monks who observed the rule of St. Benedict. Their first monastery was built near Naples, 528 A. D. The order was the most active during the tenth and eleventh centuries.

It was the first intention of the order to give instruction to those only, who were to enter upon a monastic life, but when the excellence of the instruction became known, the monks were induced to admit those who did not intend to lead such a life. Instruction was extended beyond the seven liberal arts, and included painting and poetry, and the Greek and Latin literature of the classic ages. Large libraries were founded. Benedictine nuns founded similar schools for girls, though these were not very largely attended. The rod was unsparingly used.

These schools spread rapidly. Noted ones were established in Italy, France, Switzerland, Germany and England. After the twelfth century they declined, still there are a few of them to-day. Yarrow, in England, produced the illustrious Bede, and York, the learned Alcuin. The Benedictines preserved the classics during the Middle Ages, published good editions of the Fathers, instructed the people, built universities, and fostered music, architecture and painting.

FRANCISCAN FRIARS

The Franciscan Friars were an order of the Catholic church, founded in 1182. Priests chose absolute poverty as a badge of a new apostate to carry the gospel to the poor. They went everywhere arousing the masses. They made Assisi the capital of Christian art. Their rule was carried on not in cloisters, but in the busiest haunts of man. They inspired a religious revival in the towns, which made men conscious of their ignorance and led to a desire for knowledge.

DOMINICAN FRIARS.

The order of Dominican Friars was founded at Toulouse, 1216. They lived in strict discipline and established many monasteries. They were called Black Friars in England and Jacobins in France. Their first monastery in London was in the neighborhood of what is now called Blackfriars. Their reputation is stained by the part they took in the inquisition. The Jesuits in the sixteenth century gradually took the power exercised by the Dominicans. Thomas Aquinas, (1227-1274) a noted schoolman, was the most eminent scholar belonging to the order. He was born in Naples and joined the order about 1243. After preaching with great success in Paris, he went to Rome to teach philosophy. He was a modest man, and did not seek conspicuous positions. He refused a bishopric. His greatest work is "Sum of Theology."

CHAPTER IX.

EDUCATORS OF THE MIDDLE AGES.

Charlemagne (742-814). Charlemagne, king of the Franks and a Roman Emperor, was the most active and intelligent ruler of his time. Although actively engaged in carrying on wars for forty-three years, he studied science, Latin and Greek, spread Christian teaching, and built up a vast dominion. He discussed with the Bishop deep theological questions, familiarized himself with the foremost questions of his day. He was energetic, sagacious and vigilant. He encouraged agriculture, trade, art and letters, and founded monasteries and schools.

He contemplated the organization of a popular school system. The best teachers of the land were sought after. Seeing that the clergy was the only class that could supply him with good teachers, he saw that they were thoroughly educated. Schools were organized in the monasteries, in which reading, writing, arithmetic, grammar and singing were taught. Feeling the importance of the development of language of a people, he ordered that the Lord's Prayer and the Apostles' Creed should be learned in the German tongue, but he said that God could be worshiped in the Latin and Greek tongues. The clergy were compelled to lead moral lives. Among the great scholars that he invited to his court was Alcuin of England.

ALCUIN. (735-804).

Alcuin was considered the most learned man of his age. He was born at York. He founded schools at Aix-la-Chapelle and Paris. He was the first minister of public instruction in France. The Palatine school which followed the court on its travels, was founded by him. In this he taught Charlemange and his children rhetoric, divinity, logic, and mathematics. "France is indebted to Alcuin for all the polite training of which it could boast in that and the following ages."

Alcuin's method has been likened to Socrates', but Alcuin's interrogations were not so searching as those of Socrates, nor did they call out the intelligence of the pupil as did those of the noted Greek. Alcuin's replies were good maxims with which to store the memory. He made the first attempt to form an "alliance between classical literature and Christian inspiration." He left many letters, poems, and works on theology. Some say that he founded the universities of Paris and Tours. The monastic schools that he established gave a strong impetus to the world of learning. He caused the cathedral schools to be reopened and their course of study enlarged, and restored the manuscript of the old Roman literature as text books.

ALDHELM. (——709.)

Aldhelm was related to one of the West Saxon kings. He traveled in France and Italy, and afterward studied under the renowned Hadrian in Canterbury. He was a "man of universal erudition, having an elegant style." King Alfred regarded Aldhelm the best of all the Saxon poets. His musical talents were of superior merit. He founded a school at Malmesbury, England, and opened its doors to the secular clergy and expanded its curriculum to include Latin and Greek authors.

BEDE (THE VENERABLE.) (673-735.)

The story of Bede's life is told in his own Ecclesiastical History of Britain. His education was obtained in a monastery. He became one of the most learned students of the Scriptures of his time. At nineteen he received deacon's orders; at thirty, those of the priesthood. His industry is shown by his doing the usual manual labors of the monastery, the duties of the priest, the work of a teacher and by writing upwards of forty different treatises. His "Ecclesiastical History of Britain" was written to preserve among the Anglo-Saxons the memory of their conversion to the Christian faith and to tell them of their political life.

ABELARD. (1079-1142.)

Abelard, a French philosopher, taught in many places, but largely in Paris. He sought to avoid the extremes of nominalism, the teaching that conceptions exist in name only, and realism, the teaching of real existences. He was subtle and skilled in logic, but he cared more for fame than he did for truth. His theological and philosophical writings kept the Christians of his day in high state of excitement. His influence upon the schools of the Middle Ages was great. He applied dialectics to theology and so "contributed more than any other to the foundation of scholasticism."

SUMMARY OF MIDDLE AGE EDUCATION.

1. Discipline was harsh, tending towards coarseness in manners.

2. Education was literary, the Scriptures being the chief subject of study.

3. Instruction was almost exclusively religious; it was dogmatic and exalted words over things.

4. Training was for the life to come.

5. Church and school were united.

6. Education was regarded with a spirit of seriousness.

7. Scholasticism prevailed. It led to nice discriminations and developed the powers of reasoning.

8. Learning was a process of memorizing, which stifled independent inquiry.

9. It was taught that Christianity included the whole human race, hence the intellectual enfranchisement of woman. This made primary education necessary.

10. It was shown how difficult it is to attain to symmetry and moderation in education.

CHAPTER X.

RENAISSANCE.

The renaissance was the revival of learning during the 15th and 16th centuries. The causes that led to the renaissance were: The strengthening of the governments of central Europe; the establishment of universities; numerous church councils; the invention of the art of printing; the acquaintance of different governments through diplomacy; the revival of interest in the study of the Greek literature; geographical discoveries; and a settled form of national languages; the crusaders; the invention of the mariner's compass; the breaking down of feudalism; the invention of gunpowder; and the rise of the great commercial cities.

What is known as modern education begins with the renaissance. The education of the Middle Ages was repressive, rigid, formal, severe and narrow; the revival of learning gave an education broader and more liberal. It produced a sound body for a sound mind; freed itself from the fixed form of reasoning by the schoolmen; quickened the moral sense; strove after things, not words; and attempted to develop the whole man.

The theories of education in the sixteenth century were very much in advance of the age. It is doubtful whether we have to-day, in practice, caught up with the pedagogical precepts laid down by educational writers of that century. But the attempt to attain the ideal in teaching improved the condition of the schools. An improvement has been gradual but sure since then.

Scholasticism gave way to humanistic education during this age. Scholasticism was the study of syllogistic reasoning. "The syllogism was a natural instrument of an age of faith, when men wished to demonstrate immutable dogmas, without ever making an innovation on established beliefs. It has often been observed that the art of reasoning is the science of a people in the early stage of its progress. A subtle dialect is in perfect keeping with manners still rude. It is only an intellectual machine. It is not a question of original thinking. Philosophy was but the humble servant of theology." The study of the humanities, that is, of the Greek in the original, began about 1450, the time of the conquest of Constantinople by the Turks. When the Greek empire broke up, Greek scholars carried their literature to all parts of Europe. There were serious defects in humanistic education. Its ideal was the study of words, "First, words were taught instead of things; second language was taught not as a living organic whole, fitted and completed for the service of life, but as a collection of dried specimens tabulated and arranged by the ingenuity of grammarians." Bacon, through his inductive philosophy, seems to have shown the "insufficiency of the past and the bright hopes of the future.

Humanities indicate the study of language, embracing the ancient classics, grammar, rhetoric, philology and poetry, or those studies pertaining to polite literature. The name implies that these studies have a tendency to humanize man—to make him cultured. These studies have been superseded of late by those that are deemed more practical, or more utilitarian.

Scholasticism was a name applied to the Christian philosophy of the Middle Ages. It denied philosophy the right to discuss matters out of the church, thus it led to logic and dialectics.

The schools of the humanists gave way to those of the realists. Under the humanists the dead languages and religious dogmas received undue prominence, the practical side of life was ignored, the higher institutions were advocated and the elementery schools neglected. Rabelais was the first to check this one-sided education. He was soon followed by Montaigne and Bacon. The realist advocated the teaching of things rather than words and the acquisition of practical knowledge. Natural science and physical training was added to the school curriculum and teaching underwent a marked change.

CHAPTER XI.

EDUCATORS OF THE 16TH CENTURY.

ERASMUS. (1467-1536.)

Erasmus was was born at Rotterdam. He was educated at the University of Paris, where he showed himself to be a precocious student. He was placed in a monastery that his guardians might secure his patrimony. His studies were prosecuted with diligence. His travels through England, France, and Italy brought him the acquaintance of many prominent men, who paid him the homage that was due his talents.

Erasmus did not teach, but he communicated his enthusiasm for classical literature to his contemporaries. He said, "When I have money, I will first buy Greek books and then clothes." Through his industry and studiousness, he wrote many translations and original works. Many of these pertained to secondary education. He is called therefore one of the originators of it.

At first he worked on friendly terms with Luther. Not being dogmatic, he therefore later dissented from some of the doctrines of Luther. He was egotistic, timid and undecided. He confessed, "I have no inclination to risk my life for the truth. * * * Popes and emperors must settle creeds. If they settle them well, so much the better; if ill, I shall keep on the safe side."

The reformation had a strong contributing element in Erasmus. His preaching was for tolerance and for a Christian life. He was opposed to speculative theology. He published in 1516 the New Testament in Greek, which was an important contribution to the revival of letters. He said, "It is my desire to lead back that cold dispute about words called theology to its real foundation."

Erasmus did much to improve education. He with Quintilian advocated that children should be early sent to school, that care should be given to their manners and morals and that they should acquire a choice use of language. He insists that the efforts of children should be adapted to their capacities, that they need play as well as work, that discipline should not be too severe, that the objective method be used for teaching reading and that Greek and Latin should be taught. His Colloquies is considered his best work. It is intended for the instruction of youth in Latin and in morals. His educational writings are keen and display good judgment. All imitations, with which he charged the Ciceronians, he was an enemy of. He says,"The teacher ought to explain only what is strictly necessary for understanding the author; he ought to resist the temptation of making on every occasion a display of his knowledge." He wrote "On the Order of Study"; "Of the first Liberal Education of Children."

MELANCTHON. (1497-1560.)

Melancthon, whose real name was Schwarzerd, was born at Bulten, Germany. He was early placed in the hands of a strict school-master, who taught him grammar. Through his scholarship, he won the regard of many eminent men, when he was a mere schoolboy. In 1515, he became professor of Greek in the University of Wittenberg. In this position he won deserved laurels. Luther became his devoted friend.

His influence upon the education of Germany was salutary. He was an able teacher. Students from all parts of Europe came to his instruction. His relations with his students were of the most genial kind. He says, "I can truthfully affirm that I love all the students with a fatherly affection." His text books were so clear and so superior to others written before his day that some of his were used over 100 years. He wrote the first work on dogmatic theology in the Protestant church. Luther thought this next to the Bible.

He is the author of the Saxony School Plan. This was used as the basis of school organization throughout Germany for many years. In this plan he advocated the teaching of Latin, the disuse of too many text books and the graded system. He recommended the study of Latin not German, Greek or Hebrew, that the children might learn something well. There were three grades proposed. In the first, reading, writing, Latin words, the Lord's Prayer, and the creed should be taught; in the second, grammar and Latin reading, music and explanations of the scripture and Christian duties; in the third, music and the ability to read and write Latin.

LUTHER. (1483-1546.)

One of the leading reformers of the 16th century was Martin Luther. He was born of humble parents, in a small German town. His father treated him severely. Through many trials he obtained his degree at the University of Erfurt at eighteen. Finding a Bible in the library, he decided from its perusal to lead a monastic life.

After graduation he was called to a chair in the University of Wittenberg, where he lectured upon the Bible. After seeing the profligacy of the papal court, he began to preach against it. This was the beginning of the Reformation. To answer for his doctrines, he was summoned before the imperial diet at Worms. He was urged to recant. But he said, "Unless I am proved to be in error by testimony from Holy Writ, or by clear and overpowering reasons, I can not and will not recant." This stand brought to a successful issue brought an era of personal freedom and of civil and religious liberty. He died peacefully in 1546.

The success of the reformation made the establishment of schools necessary. Luther therefore became much interested in the schools of his day. His address to the councillors of all German cities is one of the most important educational documents ever written. He taught that it is for the interest of church and of state for good schools to be supported, that it is wise for public safety to maintain family discipline, that the work of the teacher is an exalted one and that learning is a source of wealth to a community. Germany was aroused by his appeals and the foundations for popular education were laid. The immediate result of this paper was that Luther's plans for the organization of public instruction were adopted throughout Protestant Germany. New schools were established and old ones improved.

The education of girls owes its origin to this address. Universal education was established and, ever after, the state was held responsible for the education of its subjects.

"If we survey the pedagogy of Luther in all its extent and imagine it fully realized in practice, what a splendid picture the schools and education of the sixteenth century would present. We should have course of study, text-school books, teachers, methods, principles, and order of discipline, and school regulations, that could serve as models for our own age."

RABELAIS. (1483-1553.)

Rabelais, a Frenchman, was bred a Franciscan monk but afterwards became a Benedictine. He soon withdrew from these orders and became a professor of medicine, and later a corrector of texts in a printing house. To carry out educational reforms, he wrote his Life of Gargantua.

Gargantua was a giant, who was sent to school to a scholastic. After forty-five years of training, he meets a properly trained lad of twelve, Eudemon, and cries "like a cow casting down his face and hiding it with his cap." Gargantua is now properly trained, and during this training Rabelais tells what should be the subject matter of education, its method and its results; he endeavored to show that boys should be trained for the practical activities of life and be made useful citizens.

Gargantua and his teacher contemplate the beauties of the heavens evenings and observe the changes that take place there in the morning. At the table, they talk about the food upon it. In their walks, they observe everything—the flowers, the work-shops and the laborers at work. Occasionally a day is spent playing, singing, hunting, and fishing. The pupil is taught various kinds of manual labor. He is taught to engage in various games, such as ball playing, in swimming, and in rowing.

Rabelais violently opposed scholasticism; he was the first pedagogue to appear as a realist. There is such a striking contrast between the education that he advocated and the education before his day that his system is called the new education.

He advocated that teaching should be done by personal influence of the teacher and subordinately through books; teaching through the senses; training for practical life; equal development of mind and body; independence of thought and gentle treatment.

His ideas have exerted a powerful influence upon modern education. The disturbed condition of his time did not permit them to produce immediate fruit. But they bore fruit in Montaigne, Locke, Rousseau and Comenius.

JOHN STURM. (1507-1589.)

John Sturm, the rector of the Gymnasium at Strasburg for forty-five years, was born in Prussia in 1507. "His ideal of education was piety, knowledge, and eloquence. He clearly knew what he wished, and with equal clearness, he adopted means to its attainment."

His Gymnasium had in its course of study ten classes. The groundwork of the course was Latin and Greek. It was humanistic. It was carefully graded, though it was narrow in its scope. Greek and Latin were given great prominence; history, mathematics and natural science were ignored.

The gymnasium was a model for many other classical

schools in England and elsewhere to pattern after. Sturm gave a permanent form to the new education.

Sturm's method of teaching Latin and Greek was that of double translation. He advocated that subjects within range of the abilities of the pupils should be taught, that too much at a time should not be demanded of the pupils, and what is demanded should be mastered. He proposed a systematic organization for the secondary schools, with a graded series of studies covering ten years.

Sturm's teachers were compelled to know the work prescribed for the class preceding and following theirs. This brought about continuity of work.

MONTAIGNE. (1533-1592.)

Montaigne was born in France. He was at an early age placed in charge of a German tutor who spoke in Latin when talking with pupils. At an early age he held important political positions but he soon went into retirement, when he wrote his elaborate "Essays" on all varieties of subjects. The titles of some of these are "The Instruction of Children," "Pedantry," "The Affections of Fathers to their Children." His precepts are suggestive hints for reflection. They greatly influenced Rousseau and Locke.

In his essay on "Pedantry," he says, "Too much learning stifles the soul, just as planets are stifled by too much moisture and lamps by too much oil. Our pedants plunder knowledge from books and carry it on the tip of their lips just as birds carry seeds to feed their young. We only toil and labor to stuff the memory but leave the conscience and understanding unfurnished and void." These statements show how thoroughly Montaigne was dissatisfied with the pedantry of his time. He insisted that the chief object of education was not to breed grammarians and logicians, but to form men. To bring about this result, great care should be used to select a good teacher. "He should rather have an elegant than a learned head, and his manners and his judgment are of more importance than his reading."

He says, "I would understand my own language, and that of my neighbor with whom most of my business and conversation lies. No doubt Greek and Latin are very great ornaments, and of very great use; but we may buy them too dear." He was opposed to the humanistic scheme of education; he was a pronounced realist.

Montaigne was opposed to mechanical methods of teaching and to severe discipline. He advocated "Self-activity of the pupil in the use of all his powers and capabilities; things before words; judgment and understanding before memory; adaptation of instruction to the pupil's present abilities."

ROGER ASCHAM. (1515-1565.)

Roger Ascham, the father of pedagogy, received his bachelor's degree from Cambridge at the age of nineteen. As a mere boy, he excelled in Greek. He became proficient in music and penmanship. His various endowments secured for him the position of tutor to Queen Elizabeth, Queen Mary and Prince Edward, and also secured for him some high positions in the government.

He wrote the Schoolmaster, one of the first English works on pedagogy. This work deals with classical learning, and has many thoughts on punishments. He thinks that discipline, used to correct vice, does not belong to the schoolmaster. Discipline should not tend to confound moral distinctions in the mind of the young. "Hasty chiding dulls the wit and discourages diligence."

The book is chiefly devoted to a discussion of the author's method of teaching Latin. He used the double translation method, and urged that the translations from English into Latin should be compared with the original. He would have the pupil become familiar with the Latin and discover for himself the rules of syntax.

16TH CENTURY SUMMARY.

During this century scholasticism and pedantry received a check. Humanistic learning was in the ascendency. Realists had gained a strong foot-hold. The mind began to think freely. The introduction of the study of natural history and mathematics widened the range of studies. Women received better education and better attention was given to manners and morals. Instruction was adapted to the learner. The errors in the Middle Age education were checked. Principles and methods were harmonized. There was a reaction against instruction based wholly on authority. Against education of a professional character, there arose an education of a' liberal type. Secular education received attention. Formal book-knowledge gave way to informal, direct instruction from subjects. That education is a growth was gaining adherents. Teaching was becoming a training.

CHAPTER XII.

EDUCATORS OF THE 17th CENTURY.

RAITCH. (1571-1625.)

Raitch was a German. He devoted much study to Hebrew, Arabic and mathematics. He offered a new method of teaching to the German Diet at Frankfort. His method, when he put it into practice, did not meet with success. He advocated that the pupil should get the formal rules of grammar through the study of good authors. This is learning a language from the concrete to the abstract, which method has had many advocates from his time down to our own. He is said to be the forerunner of Comenius.

His methods failed, not because of the lack of their excellency, but because of the character of the man He declared that he "would only sell his discoveries to a prince at a dear rate," and that when sold they should be concealed by the purchaser. He was boastful, conceited, and without influence with men. Some of his principles: 1. In all teaching follow the order and course of nature. 2. Teach only one thing at a time. 3. Often repeat the same thing. 4. Learn everything first in the mother tongue. 5. Learn nothing by heart. 6. Teach everything by experience and inquiry.

FRANCIS BACON. (1561-1626.)

Francis Bacon was born in London, the son of the Lord-Keeper of the Great Seal. Under the influence of parents who displayed dignity, intellect and refinement, in the elegance of a palace and amid cultured associates, he had an excellent opportunity to cultivate his refined tastes. At thirteen he entered Cambridge, where he received a lasting contempt for the impractical studies of that institution. Here he saw students that were like "becalmed ships, that never move, but by the wind of other men's breath."

He was not content with teaching that did not appear palpable to him. Finding that the secrets of nature could be learned from nature only, he broke with the scholastic routinists. His researches were made from original investigation. He discovered important principles in natural science and mathematics.

After leaving college, he successively traveled, studied law and entered parliament. During this time he published a volume of Essays which are classic. Under James I., he held many important political positions. His life at the court is not without criticism. He was truckling and ungrateful to friends. He was thrown into the Tower for taking bribes, but soon obtained his release. His later days were spent in poverty and repentance, but in literary activity.

Bacon's work has had a powerful effect on education. He advocated that the true method of teaching proceeds from observation of the facts of nature..

Scholasticism received a death-blow from Bacon. For several centuries before his time, there were indications that the age of false premises and futile reasoning was drawing to a close. Thought was advancing; Bacon came to give direction to it.

Bacon is the author of the inductive method. He desired man to become "the minister and interpreter of nature." He showed, through his greatest work—Instruatio Magna, how induction should be carried into different lines of inquiry. Investigation, experiment, verification, are characteristic features of Bacon's philosophy. "It is intensely practical; it has been potent in turning modern thought into new channels, and has contributed largely to the scientific and material progress of the present." Before Bacon's time thought was active; he made it useful.

Macaulay says, "Two words form the key of the Baconian doctrine—utility and progress. His philosophical views aimed to make science minister to the worldly wants of mankind."

COMENIUS. (1592-1671.)

Comenius was born in Moravia, Austria, of parents who belonged to the Moravian Brethren. While young he lost his parents. Up to sixteen he received instruction in reading, writing, arithmetic and the catechism. He then prepared for college. He was graduated from the University of Heidelberg. In the Thirty Years' war he lost all his property. He fled the country and found employment in the Moravian Gymnasium. Raitch and Bacon were perused, among other great educators.

As a result of this study, he wrote his Didactica-Magna, a profound study of education, and the fundamental principles of which are: (1) That all instruction must be carefully graded; (2) that, in imparting knowledge to children, the teacher must appeal to the faculties of sense perception.

Comenius' principle of gradation includes the school, the pupils, and the text-books. He divides school life into four periods of six years each. The first stage is called the mother school and begins as soon as the child leaves the cradle. The second is called the vernacular school and lays the foundation for the work that follows. The third is called the Latin school; this corresponds to the secondary school of to-day. The pupil continues the subjects taught in the varnacular school and begins the classics. The last is called the university and allows the pupil to intensify any subject that he wants to make a specialty of. His method of teaching Latin is in his Gate of Tongues Unlocked. In this he advocates, "The human being tends to utter what he apprehends. If he does not apprehend the word he uses, he is a parrot." Since the classical authors are too difficult, he composed a collection of common phrases, well graded, to be learned and used by the student. He insisted upon a study of the mother-tongue as of greater importance than the study of Latin, and declared that the study of a language to be a means, not an end.

He was invited to England, Sweden and Hungary to explain his methods of teaching to representatives of those countries. Oxenstiern of Sweden, he greatly impressed. He remained in Hungary four years, and established a model school at Patak.

These were years of great literary activity with Comenius. The most famous work of all his writings, Orbis Pictus, was written at this time. This was a popular text-book in Europe for many years. It contained "the pictures and names of all the principal things in the world, and of all the principal occupations of men." It was the first illustrated school-book ever published. Comenius says in its preface; "There is nothing in the understanding which was not before in the senses, and therefore to exercise the senses well in rightly perceiving the difference of things, will be to lay the grounds for all wisdom, and all right discourse and all discreet action in one's course of life."

Some of the principles to show that Comenius is rightfully called an educational reformer:

1. Education is a development of the whole man. 2. Educational methods should follow the order of nature. 3. Studies should be adapted to the capacity of the pupil. 4. Discipline should aim at improving character. 5. Words should be learned in connection with things. 6. It is the aim of education so to direct and control the development of man's innate powers that he may fulfill his destiny wisely and conscientiously. 7. All must be educated,—universal education. 8. We must learn to do by doing—a rule for teaching.

He returned from Hungary to his home at Lissa in 1654. The Poles in 1656 sacked the town. He lost all of his valuable manuscripts and library. He said, "This loss I shall cease to lament only when I cease to breathe." He was then invited to Amsterdam where he spent the rest of his life writing, in the home of Laurence De Geer. Here he published a complete edition of his works. He exhibited in all his misfortunes a meek, Christian spirit.

JOHN LOCKE. (1632-1704.)

John Locke's father was an officer in the civil war of England. He early entered Oxford, and like Bacon received a lasting contempt for the educational practices there. He studied medicine but did not practice it. In its study he made praiseworthy advancement. He was early thrown in contact wth people of rank, but he did not lose his independence of character.

He became instructor in the household of the Earl of Shaftesbury. Through this experience his attention was directed toward education. His Essay concerning Human Understanding was regarding the limitations and capabilities of the mind. What Bacon had done to investigate the principles of induction as applied to external nature, Locke did in his investigation of the mind of man. "He established the important doctrine that there are no innate principles in the mind, and that all ideas come from sensation or reflecton, from external or internal reflecton."

His greatest pedagogical work is Thoughts on Education. It has special reference to the educaton of noblemen. In it, he strongly advocates private instruction; it has no claim as a system of universal education. He regards health and virtue more important than learning, but learning an aid to virtue and wisdom. According to him education in its widest sense is the moulding force of life. As against bookish learning, he taught "The function of education was to form noble men well equipped for the duties of practical life." Other thoughts from this essay are, "There ought very early to be imprinted on his [pupil's] mind a true notion of God. Plenty of open air, exercise and sleep; plain diet, no wine or strong drink; not too warm and straight clothing. He that is about children should study their natures and aptitudes. The exercises imposed upon pupils should be wisely adjusted to their powers and attainments. The mother-tongue has the highest claims upon us. A knowledge of Latin is overrated . The best way to learn a language is by practice, not by rule." According to Quick, "Locke's aim was to give a boy a robust mind in sound body. * * * His spirits were to be kept up by kind treatment, and learning was never to be a drudgery. * * * In everything the part the pupil was to play in life was steadily to be kept in view; and the ideal which Locke proposed was not the finished scholar, but the finished gentleman."

FENELON. (1651-1715.)

Fenelon was remarkable for industry, intelligence and amiability. He was taught in his home until twelve years of age. Soon after this he went to Paris where he took a complete course of instruction. He studied theology, in which he won distinction. At an early age he was placed at the head of a Catholic institution in Paris for the education of women.

At the request of the Duke and the Dutchess of Beauvillers, who had eight daughters to educate, Fenelon wrote his treatise On the Education of Girls. In it he points out the faults in the education of women, the principles and methods in the education of boys as well as of girls, and the duties and the studies of women. He says that women should be excluded from politics, law, and the minstry. Since woman has in her hands the details of domestic matters, she has the principal part in the good or bad morals of the world. Man cannot establish measures for good unless he has woman to aid him in their execution. Woman's education is a necessity, since "ignorant and idle girls have wandering imagination," turning curiosity to "vain and dangerous subjects." The education should begin at an early age and be pleasant.

"Let wisdom be forced upon him only at intervals." Girls should be instructed in reading, writing, arithmetic, history, language, music, painting, in justice and government

To instruct Louis XIV., a headstrong child, he wrote an admirable series of thirty-six Fables and seventy-nine Dialogues, and the Adventures of Telemachus. This mode of instruction, he called indirect instruction.

The Fables show the bad uses to which unlimited power may be employed, the evil effects of bad temper, and many such suggestive instruction to correct the faults of the young prince. The Dialogues of the Dead relate the conversations in the region of the dead, of historic personages. These were intended to teach the young prince important facts of history and how to become a good and wise king. The Adventures of Telemachus relates how the son of Ulysses searched for his father, and how he learned to govern justly under the direction of Minerva, in the guise of Mentor.

Fenelon shows that education is a moulding force, that nature and art play an important part in teaching, that educaton may be a pastime, that fables may inculcate great moral lessons, that the instincts of a child are to be directed not repulsed, that a child should not be overcrowded, and that discretion should be used in the selection of matters to be taught.

THE JESUITS OR SOCIETY OF JESUS.

The Jesuit schools were established by Ignatius Loyola in the 16th century. They checked the progress of the reformation. In western Europe they were numerous and their influence was beneficent. Protestants as well as Catholics flocked to them. The teachers were men of marked ability and consecrated to the interests of the school. The preparation for their work was long and painstaking. A daily preparation of their lessons was exacted and a careful supervision of their work was maintained.

Loyola realized that "enthusiasm for the Order of Jesus must come from a source of power. * * * He fostered, therefore, a consciousness of strength. His clergy, he determined, should be made truly learned. * * The education, on the contrary, was to be made elaborately superficial, in order to give them that variety of learning which is the best safeguard against real thought and progressive study. [In this way] he created a medium, favorable to the influence of the astute minds of the clergy."

Loyola's plan was greatly modified by other wise leaders of the Society. "The child, in their scheme, is not to be brought to his own perfection, but is to be moulded into a symmetrical and unchangeable pillar of the Jesuit Order. He is not to become , not a human temple, but an infinitesimal fraction of the church Jesuitical."

The course of study consisted of ancient classics, philosophy and theology. In the lower of the two courses, arithmetic, history and natural science were taught and by teachers not belonging to the order. In the higher course, the best teachers were employed. The methods adopted were uniform and agreeable and adapted to the capacity of the pupil taught. The teaching was largely oral. Emulation was appealed to in the form of badges, prizes, etc. An excellent knowledge of Latin was obtained.

The Jesuits were very successful because they did not have an elaborate course and what they taught they taught well. Their chief purpose was to give a good Latin style. Then the spirit of emulation was thoroughly aroused. In school pupils competed for rewards of different kinds, and public festivals were held to exhibit the pupils and to flatter parents.

Those who criticise them say that they were narrow in their application of education and questionable in motive. "Nothing shows more clearly the essential weakness of their system than its inadaptability to modern wants."

But we can say in favor of the Jesuits that they were good schoolmasters, took care of the physical training and good manners of their pupils, were pioneers in the training of their teachers for the work and in providing supervision of the work while in progress, were the founders of many excellent colleges, still in existence, thoroughly trained the memory by frequent reviews and dissertations, and used the class-teaching system, which required the teacher to teach all subjects in a class and to take his pupils through several or all of the classes.

THE PORT-ROYALISTS (JANSENISTS.) (1643-1660.)

The schools of Port Royal, near Paris, were founded by Saint Cyran. He said, "Education is, in a sense, the one thing necessary. I wish you might read in my heart the affection I feel for children." This was a characteristic feeling of the Jansenists for the work of teaching. These schools were started apparently to check the evil tendencies of the Jesuits, and therefore met with such persecution from that strong organization tha they existed but seventeen years.

They discouraged emulation, gave to each teacher but

five or six pupils and did not "forget the reverence due to the indwelling, to the Holy Spirit." The pupils' studies were in French, not in the Latin language; their work was made agreeable. Steel pens were invented for the use of the children. Pupils were directed to "speak little, bear much, pray more." Lessons were often given in the open air.

The Jansenists became very influential through the text-books that they wrote. Nicole wrote a text-book in which he recommended the training of the senses and of the heart. Constel wrote Rules of Education for Children, and Arnauld, Elements of Geometry.

The "little schools" of the Jansenists, as they were called, trained but a few hundred children, but their spirit pervaded the whole of France. Their text-books were models for their enemies even.

The Jansenists aimed at thoroughness, studied language to give full meaning to truth, more than the form of the classical authors, based their teaching upon the mother-tongue, were free from pedantry, and gave an impulse to the study of the principles of Bacon.

THE ORATORIANS. (1614.)

The Oratorians were founded by Berulle in France in 1614. This order was friendly to the Jansenists. It attempted to found an education, liberal and Christian. The Oratorians were sincere lovers of truth. In spite of the opposition given by the Jesuits, they grew in influence. In fifteen years after its foundation, they had more than fifty houses or colleges. They took no part in politics. They promoted a study of their mother tongue. The study of geography was united with that of history. Both were enlivened by the use of wall charts. Two noted writers of the order were Lamy and Fleury.

17TH CENTURY SUMMARY.

The reformers of the 17th century insisted that nothing should be memorized that is not understood; went from the simple and obvious to the complex, keeping in view the growing powers of the child, thus making the acquisition of knowledge agreeable, and largely doing away with punishments; cultivated the power of observation; and taught subjects that will be useful in life. Advance steps were made in mathematics. Letters were used to represent known quantities, principles pertaining to exponents, positive and negative roots were introduced by Descartes, and the calculus was invented by Newton and Leibnitz. Believing that the Greeks had exhausted all scientific knowledge, the reformers strove for a mastery of the Greek and Latin authors. Education was largely ecclesiastical. The influence of noted philosophers, such as Bacon, was felt. The education of girls was promoted. American education had its beginning.

CHAPTER XIII.

EDUCATORS OF THE 18TH CENTURY.

ROUSSEAU. (1712-1778.)

One of the men who has exerted the greatest influence over the destinies of pedagogy is Rousseau. He was born in Geneva, the son of a watchmaker. The sensitive fancy of his childhood was fed on romances, which he says he thoroughly felt. He was first an attorney and then an engraver, both of which positions he soon left in disgust. He successively changed his religious faith, entered the service of a nobleman who gave him some education, and then lived with Mme. de Warens, where he studied zealously philosophy and politics. Losing her favor, he went to Lyons, where he tutored two boys. As a teacher, he was a failure, for he had such a hasty temper that he could not control himself and certainly not his pupils.

He lost the favor of Catholics and Protestants, because of alleged heresy and immorality. He fled to England, where he was kindly received by Hume. Quarreling with him, he returned to France.

"His life was a singular paradox. .. .. This man, who wrote admirable pages upon domestic affection, friendship and gratitude, chose a companion unworthy of him, placed his children in a foundling hospital, and showed himself unjust and harsh toward his friends. All the time doing wrong, he believed himself moral, because he loved virtue."

Rousseau's reputation as an author rests upon his Emile. The work shows the influence of Montaigne and Rabelais on its author. It shows a keen insight into child nature and the shortcomings of his day. There are five sections in the book, dealing with earliest childhood, up to Emile's twelfth year, to his fifteenth, to his twentieth and up to marriage. Education is not to make a citizen, but a man. Nature, men and things are the educating influences.

In Emile, the author sets forth in detail the matter and method of teaching. Some of the truths in it are: People do not understand childhood; nature requires children to be children. The child must learn to feel warmth and coldness, the hardness, softness and weight of bodies; to judge of their figure, magnitude and other sensible qualities. Too much reading serves only to make us presumptous blockheads. By the developing method, we do not accustom ourselves to a servile submission to the authority of others. All the education of women ought to be relative to that of men. He pays a glowing tribute to the gospel of Christ.

Rousseau starts out in Emile with the statement that "all is good as it issues from the hands of the author of all things; everything degenerates in the hands of man." He repeatedly talks about restoring the child "to the state of nature." The successive stages of education are: (1) Education of the body and senses (till twelfth year); (2) intellectual education (to the fifteenth year); (3) moral education (to the twentieth year). The intellectual education should be utilitarian—the study of the practical arts and sciences. Moral education should be sentimental, and religious education should be delayed to prevent superstitious feelings.

Rousseau did not strive to give an education that would prove a panacea for all evils. He wrote: "An education of a certain kind may be practicable in Switzerland, but not in France; one kind of education may be best for the middle class, and another for the nobility."

The underlying current of Emile is, "Freedom; liberation from the bonds of a degenerated civilization; destruction of traditional prejudices and abuses; respect for human individuality; equality before the assizes of society and political organization; return from the darkness of intolerance, on the one hand, and hideous atheism on the other, to the light of reason, simplicity of faith, and an all embracing charity."

BASEDOW. (1723-1790.)

Basedow belonged to a group of educators known as philanthropinists, named after the first school founded by them. The philanthropinists sought to correct the improper instruction of their time. They advocated everything according to nature. Comenius, Locke and Rousseau greatly influenced them.

Basedow was born at Hamburg. His father was a stern man, who did not at first see the promise of his son. When he did see it, he was sent to school at a gymnasium. Later he went to Leipsic, where he studied theology. His heterodox ideas debarred him from his destined profession. As tutor and professor his heterodox ideas put him under a special ban and excluded him from the communion.

In 1768, he published his School Studies. His

elementary book was a kind of Orbis Pictus, intending to teach morals, nature, duties of citizens, and business. He applied the theories of Rousseau on his daughter Emilie. She at five was able to speak French, Latin and German and was fond of domestic duties.

In 1774, he founded his Philanthropinum, where he experimented with the methods of Rousseau, Locke and Comenius. He undertook to teach children a language in a year. To shorten the work of learning, he says that all text books should be put in such relations with each other that one shall shorten or lengthen another. His school rose rapidly and fell as rapidly. He strove to overcome the dull routine of school work and the gloomy surroundings of pupils prevalent in his day, by taking proper care of body, soul and mind. His methods of moral instruction were "an elaborate ceremonial." Many books have been written to disseminate his ideas. The "Swiss Family Robinson" is one of these. He followed nature in all things, gave careful training to the body, guided the pupil by love, appealed to direct observation, and encouraged manual work and dress that would give freedom to the body.

His book of methods gives faithfully his pedagogical opinions. He says that the public and domestic education is not adapted to the needs of the times. To bring about the required adaptability, he says that new text books must be written and teachers' training schools must be established. He declares that the aim of an education should be "to prepare children for a useful, patriotic and happy life." Instruction from things must really furnish the intellect with new ideas, and not fill up the child's memory with new words only. * * * Few words and much doing."

What philanthropinism has done for pedagogy: It attempted to raise pedagogy to a science; it secured physical culture as a part of the school discipline; it employed illustrative teaching in place of memory cramming; it made school-rooms cheerful by placing in them loving friends in place of despots; it banished the whip and ferrule; it introduced hygienic dress; it advocated manual training.

18TH CENTURY SUMMARY.

The 18th century began under favorable auspices. Bacon, Sir Isaac Newton and other thinkers of the 17th century gave their influences to the reformers of the 18th. But this century, marked with political and social unrest, was a period of fermentation, which bore its fruit for the next age. Some of the characteristic phases of the education of this century were its spiritual character as set fort by Francke, its utilitarian tendencies, the professional training of teachers, its interest in pedagogic questions, the more liberal spirit with the universities, the beginning of the work of Pestalozzi, the growth of popular education in Germany, education tended to become national and humane, and education aimed at the most complete development of the individual order.

The humanistic movement of the eighteenth century made the classics of antiquity the basis of culture. It was a reaction against the realists, represented by Rousseau and the philanthropinists; "(1) Humanism aims at general culture; philanthropinism at utility. (2) Humanism seeks to exercise and strengthen the mind; philanthropinism to fill it with useful knowledge. (3) Humanism demands but few subjects of study; philanthropinism many. (4) Humanism exercises the mind with ideas; philanthropinism with things. (5) Humanism deals with the true, the beautiful, and the good, the elements of human culture; philanthropinism, with matter." Representatives of humanistic learning in the eighteenth century were Wolf, Gesner and Heyne.

CHAPTER XIV.

EDUCATORS OF THE 19TH CENTURY.

PESTALOZZI. (1746-1827.)

Pestalozzi was born at Zurich, Switzerland. At the age of five he lost his father, when he was thrown under the influence of a good mother, but he kept himself so completely in the narrow confinement of his mother's chamber that the real life of men was as strange to him as if he had not lived in the world. He was called by his mates "Wonderful Harry from fool's town."

Pestalozzi studied for the ministry but after reading Rousseau's Emile, he decided to study law that he might be of greater usefulness to his country. This change proved a failure. At Neuhof, he determined to devote himself to agriculture. This enterprise was a failure. Still under the influence of Emile, he opened an industrial school for the poor. In this work he was greatly assisted by his estimable wife. But in five years the school was closed. The children were unaccustomed to discipline, and would often run away as soon as they were decently clothed. He was patient with them all, and "lived like a beggar to teach beggars how men live."

His first work was The Evening Hours of a Recluse. It contains principles of education. Education in the family, knowledge of things, and love in the home are some of the thoughts discussed. The work that made him famous was his Leonard and Gertrude. He received as a result of its publication medals from educational societies and letters of praise from princes. It was written "to bring about a better education for the people, arising out of their true position and their natural circumstances." Gertrude, the wife of the weak-minded Leonard, is a model mother. Pestalozzi tells how Gertrude manages her home and brings up her children. He tried to supply the want of good schools to educate properly the young by giving to the mothers such principles of teaching as would enable them to bring up their children as well as they could if they possessed a knowledge of all the sciences.

During the French revolution, Stanz, with many other Swiss towns was burned. Many orphans were without a home. Pestalozzi became a father to eighty of these between four and ten years of age. He found the children in all states of wretchedness. He tried to combine learning with handiwork. He saw the condition of the children change "as winter is changed to spring by the action of the sun." He says, "my tears flowed with theirs and my smile accompanied theirs. * * * I slept in their midst; I was the last to go to bed at evening and the first to rise in the morning." After nine months, the French returned and turned his school building into a hospital. In 1801 he wrote "How Gertrude Teaches her Children." In 1802, he went to Yverdun, and established a school which received a national reputation.

Pestalozzi was the author of what is known as object teaching; i. e., teaching by means of visible objects. Some of the features of the Pestalozzian instruction are: The mind of the child should be developed through his and experience; the child's mind should be furnished with clear fundamental notions; truth should be presented to the child objectively; instruction should proceed from the known to the unknown, from the near to the more remote; mental should be associated with manual labor; the relation between teacher and pupil should be love; character should be the standard of instruction; and home instruction should be possible.

Fitch says, "Oliver Wendell Holmes once said of Emerson that he was an iconoclast without the hammer; that the idols he sought to dethrone he took down from their pedestals so quietly and reverently that he seemed more like one performing an act of worship. In some sense this is true of Pestalozzi. He, too, was an iconoclast, but he went about his work in a very different spirit from that which animated Rousseau to whom he was in other respects nearly akin. * * * There is in Pestalozzi little or no denunciation; none of the fierce revolt against established notions and usages which characterized Rousseau; only an earnest appeal to parents and teachers—all the more effectual because so restrained and modest—to follow books and traditions less and to study nature and childhood more."

Rosenkranz says of the pedagogic achievements of Pestalozzzi: "(1) In the method of instruction, he has substituted for the artificial and playful modes of procedure, the striving after the cheerful seriousness resulting from, and embodied in, the form of development given by nature herself.

(2) He has emancipated the government of children from all terrorism. In place of compulsion and lifeless mechanism, he has put the most loving treatment of pupil, in order to habituate him to self-activity and self-esteem.

(3) He has opened our eyes to the fact that all culture of individual intelligence and all moral elevation of the individual will are vain in the end if they do not issue forth from out of the whole spirit of a people and do not flow back into it as its original property. He has taught us to regard education essentially as a national education."

Summary: Pestalozzi is regarded as the founder of modern pedagogics. He has had a powerful influence on elementary education. His principles underlie all primary schools of to-day. Froebel further developed them practically and Herbart theoretically. Rosenkranz was his disciple and Herbert Spencer, one of his most illustrious followers.

FROEBEL. (1782-1852.)

Frederick Froebel was born in a small town in Germany. His mother died when he was a baby and his father was too busy a pastor to give his boy any attention. While watching workmen repairing a church from his nursery window, he received the impulse to devise materials for children's playthings for instructive purposes. He could not get interested in the formal lessons of the old school and was therefore pronounced dull. He entered the University at Jena at 18, but soon left for lack of means and because he did not become interested in the instruction given. While at Frankfort, he was made teacher in a normal school. He now felt that he was in his proper element.

He heard of Pestalozzi at Yverdun. His enthusiasm was thoroughly kindled. In 1815· he established a school at Keilhau, where self activity might be connected with manual labor. After a varied experience of fifteen years, he became convinced that the time had come when a change in the methods of instruction should be made. He then founded the Kindergarten, upon which his fame rests. He said, "I can convert children's activities, energies, amusements, occupations, all that goes by the name of play, into instruments for my purpose, and therefore transform play into work. This work will be education in the true sense of the term. These children have taught me how I am to teach them."

The Kindergarten receives children at an early age, gives direction to their ideas, develops their powers harmoniously and prepares them for the ordinary school.

Its purpose is thus indicated by Froebel himself: "To take the oversight of children before they are ready for school life; to exert an influence over their whole being in correspondence with its nature; to strengthen their bodily powers; to exercise their senses; to employ the awakening mind; make them thoroughly acquainted with the world of nature and of men; to guide their heart and soul in a right direction, and lead them to the origin of all life and union with Him."

The kindergarten is no school in the true meaning of that term; it is a "childe's garden," in which children may exercise their natural taste, where there are no text books, but where there is activity—"activity of the limbs, activity of the senses, activity of the mind, heart and of the religious instinct. It is not an infant school where children are sent to get them out of the way." Play, therefore, has its educating influence. "The child, through the spontaneous activity of all his natural forces, is really developing and strengthening them for future uses; he is working out his own education."

Note in Froebel the thoughtful student of child life: "I see that those children delight in movement. I see that they observe. I see that they invent." "Play is desultory education." He organizes the self-activities of children as a basis, on which to build the future superstructure.

Froebel's gifts are the implements used for the exercise of the intellectual faculties. Games, songs and gifts are employed in the Kindergarten system. His principal work is the Education of Man. It treats of the child preceding his kindergarten age and gives many hints to guide the mother, who is nature's deputy, in her treatment of him. Compayre says of it: "The introduction is the most interesting part of it. The idea of general phylosophy is. 'Everything comes solely from God.' Frobel is logically brought to this psychological statement, that everything is good in man, for it is God who acts in him. The pedagogical conclusion is: Education shall be essentially a work of liberty and spontaneity."

Leading ideas in Froebel's educational system:

"(1) As the child's development begins with its first breath, so must its education also.

(2) He desires for human education and instruction a developing method, education accordng to nature's laws.

(3) The spiritual and physical development are closely bound up in each other.

(4) The instincts of the child, as a being destined to become reasonable, express not only physical but also spiritual wants. Education has to satisfy both.

(5) He wants as end of human education, a life harmonious on all sides with God, men and nature."

JACOTOT. (1770-1840.)

Joseph Jacotot was a noted French educator. He was born in Dijon, and died in Paris. He was a Greek and Latin professor at Dijon, was appointed by Napoleon to a chair of mathematics in a normal school, afterwards was secretary to the minister of war and later a directo of the polytechinc school. In 1818, he was lecturer on French literature in the University of Louvin. In Belgium, he taught French to pupils who spoke nothing but Dutch and Flemish. It was here that his so-called universal method was expanded and applied.

This method contemplated theCorrelation of all knowledge. Some fact is thoroughly learned by long contemplation and observation; this becomes the key to the acquisition to other facts. This requires close attention and concentration, and develops innate powers of the pupil. He placed in the hands of the pupils at Louvin a copy of Telemachus, with the French on one page and the Dutch translation on the other, and required them to get the meaning of the text and to recite in French. They were required, by skillful questions from the teacher, to correct their own errors. Pupils, in this way, were led to educate themselves. His method followed the order of learning, repeating, comparing, and verifying. Comparison and verification demanded intellectual activity of the pupil.

He enunciated several maxims, which are seemingly paradoxes. "All human beings are equally capable of learning. Everyone can teach; and, moreover, can teach that which he does not know himself. All is in all." For a thorough discussion of these maxims, the reader is referred to Quick's Educational Reformers.

THOMAS ARNOLD. (1795-1842.)

Thomas Arnold, losing his father while quite young, received a careful education from his mother and aunt. He was graduated from Oxford with honor. While preparing to publish some of his works, his studies and discussion of religious topics, he became convinced that the noblest life is to be found in the Christian ideal. His success as a teacher is attributable to his religious spirit

In 1828, he became head-master of Rugby, and his record here is one of the most brilliant to be found in the history of teaching. His success here was "due to his own earnest endeavor to apply the principles of Christianity to life in the school as well as out of it." His devotion to Christian principle had an unbounded influence on his boys in school. The boys at Rugby were ashamed to tell Dr. Arnold a lie. If a boy attempted to explain a statement, the doctor would say, "If you say so, that is quite enough. Of course I believe your word." "Tom Brown at Rugby" gives a good picture of one of the best schools that England has ever had.

Arnold changed the nature of public school education in England. He showed that school teaching is not to be despised and that a schoolmaster should be a man of first-rate powers and should be respected. He introduced a higher moral tone into the school; his school sermons imparted a religious life to his pupils. He gave a new impetus to the classics. He had an intimate acquaintance with each pupil. He made the school a place of training for life, a place where the teacher must develop in the scholar a good will. The possibility of a manly piety was shown in his school.

His influence was great, because he was so wholehearted, so true in all that he did. His sympathies with boys made him a real leader of them. One of his pupils has said, "I always felt that Dr. Arnold was one of the greatest and best men, for whom I would have made any effort, for whom I used to think I would gladly die. I felt, too, that there was work for me to do for him in the school, and to this end I would labor to raise the tone of the set I lived in, particularly as regarded himself."

He was governed by two main principles—"as a trainer of character, he aimed to make his pupils Christian gentlemen, as a trainer of mind, to make them think."

HERBERT SPENCER. (1820—

Herbert Spencer came from a family of teachers. His father wrote a text-book on geometry, which was used many years. At seven he could not read; he enjoyed games, rambling, etc. His father encouraged him to gather insects, to watch their transformation and to make drawings of insects gathered. He was frequently disobedient. His father's library was quite an attraction to him.

Science, according to Spencer, is the chief staple of an education. The test of the worth of an education is determined by the way in which one treats the body and mind, arranges his business, brings up a family and behaves as a citizen. Science helps to get a livelihood and to make money; it trains for citizenship. The process of self-development should be encouraged to the utmost. Instruction should excite interest. Intellectual activity is not to be sacrificed to routine.

He became interested in the theory of evolution, as explaining the cause of the diversity in the animal kingdom. His views are reflected in his only educational work, Education. This confirms the conclusions made by Montaigne, Locke, Rousseau, and others. He attempts to lay down a scheme of education according to his views of evolution. He argues that the study of science aids in teaching the concrete before the abstract and gives interest to study, that corporal punishment and rote-teaching should be abandoned, and that mental growth by inherent power is superior to artificial expansion produced by purely exterior forces.

Herbert Spencer "shows that growth is organic, subject to the ordinary laws of organic development. Thus, he made psychology strictly a natural science, to be henceforth modified, extended in its scope, corrected in its errors, limited in its theories, by the same laws of criticism that apply to other natural sciences. Availing himself of the discovery of the laws of evolution, of the correlation, the indestructibility, and unstability of forces, of their inseparability from matter, he has built up a system of psychology, which * * * is destined * * to become one of the most potent agencies in hastening the recognition of correct principles of education."

BAIN. (1818——)

Alexander Bain was born in Scotland and was graduated from college in 1840. He occupied college chairs at different times and always with success. He published at different times good educational works; among them are Mental and Moral Science. Education as a Science.

He discusses most instructively the law of the conservation and correlation of forces. He says that "man has so much vital force, which may be expended in labor, in intellectual effort, or in emotion; but that which is used in one way cannot be used in another." Shoup says that "this statement is recommended to the consideration of those who teach that manual labor is a rest from study, and study a rest from work—that sawing wood is an admirable means of repose for man or boy exhausted by manual application."

Bain's writings on education are very valuable. "Perhaps the most interesting part of them consists in his showing how what may be called correlation of forces in man helps us to a right education. From this we learn that emotion may be transferred into intellect, that sensation may exhaust the brain as much as thought, and we may infer that the chief duty of the schoolmaster is to stimulate the powers of each brain under his charge to the fullest activity, and to apportion them in that ratio which will best conduce to the most complete and harmonious development of the individual."

HORACE MANN. (1796-1859.)

Horace Mann was born in Franklin, Massachusetts. He lost his father when a mere boy. His mother did not enter into the sympathies of the boy. He had few books and poor instructors. Theology to him was at an early age a burden, but later he took a bright view of Christianity. His habits were spotless. He aspired to do good to mankind. He was graduated from Brown University after three years' work there. He studied law, but was soon called to teach Latin and Greek in Brown.

In 1837, he became secretary of the board of education of Massachusetts; in this position he did the work of his life. His twelve reports are educational classics. The fifth was especially noted. It gives "the advantages of education, the effects of it upon the futures of men, the production of property, and the multiplication of human comforts." He was instrumental in establishing a normal school at Lexington, the first in the state, and the first teachers' institute.

Mann says, "In a social and political sense, ours is a free school system. It knows no distinction of rich and poor, of bond and free, or between those who in the imperfect light of this world are seeking through different avenues to reach the gate of Heaven. Without money and without price, it throws open its doors, and spreads the table of its bounty for all the children of the state."

A record of what Mann did for the schools of Massachusetts is difficult to equal. Under his direction and advice, two millions of dollars was assessed for the school buildings; teachers' salaries were doubled; the quality of teaching was vastly improved; text-books were adapted to practical instruction and became uniform; pupils were classified and well graded; normal schools and teachers' institutes were established; supervision more systematic and intelligent; and the state was made to feel that its strength lies in general education.

Mann's writings show that he was an educational reformer. They do not contain formally stated pedagogical principles. This is accounted for, by his being an educator by instruction rather than by training. He says, "Acquirement and pleasure should go hand in hand. The mind acquires, by a glance of the eye, what volumes of books and months of study could not reveal so livingly through the eye. Other things being equal, the pleasure which a child enjoys, in studying or contemplating, is proportioned to the liveliness of his perceptions and ideas. Error becomes the consequence of seeing only parts of the truth. [Hence 'no scrap-book' method of teaching reading.] A lofty and enduring character cannot be formed by ignorance and chance."

DAVID P. PAGE. (1810-1848.)

David P. Page was born in New Hampshire on a farm. A love for books was early shown, though he was restrained from attending an academical school at an early age by his father, who desired his son to be a farmer. During a severe sickness, the father, however, relented and sent the boy to Hampton Academy.

The year following he taught at Newbury, Mass. His success was marked. He went to his classes with thoroughly prepared lessons, thus imparting to his pupils fresh information. He adapted his instruction to the capacities of his pupils, and aroused their aspirations for purity and goodness.

He was an active member of teachers' associations, and his papers before them were pronounced superior in every particular. In 1844 he was made principal of the first normal school in New York state, at Albany. His success here was immediate, but the work to make the school so was too much for his health, and he sank into his grave in 1848. He had "the happy talent of always saying the right thing at the right time. He was more than ordinarily prepossessing—of good height and fine form, erect, and dignified in manner, scrupulously neat in person and easy in address." His principal work is "Theory and Practice of Teaching," one of the most valuable contributions to pedagogical literature.

David Page obtained his schooling in Hampton academy, yet he has never had a superior as teacher, in the teaching profession. He would have graced a position in any college at thirty-eight years of age—his age at the time of his death. Henry Barnard has said, "As a teacher, he exhibited two valuable qualifications,—the ability to turn the attention of his pupils to the principles which explain facts, and in such a way that they could see clearly the connection; and the talent for reading the character of his scholars, so accurately, that he could at once discern what were their governing passions and tendencies—what in them needed encouragement and what repression."

HENRY BARNARD. (1811-1898.)

Henry Barnard was graduated from Yale in 1830, and was admitted to the bar in 1836. As a member of the Connecticut legislature, he secured the passage of the act for the common schools, under which the State Board of Commissioners was organized. Mr. Barnard's duties as secretary of this board was to disseminate information and to devise means for improvement of the schools. The reports of Mr. Barnard were helpful. He was called to Rhode Island where he did a similar service for that state. He was made principal of the New Britain, Conn., normal school, in 1849. This was the third one in the United States.

His American Journal of Education is his most noted work. This was established in 1855. At first it appeared monthly, later quarterly. Each number contains about 200 pages and gives educational biography, and national and foreign school systems. "Upon the whole, no American journal devoted to education has had a more general or salutary influence upon the higher education, or has done more to dignify the cause of liberal culture." He was appointed in 1867 the first United States Commissioner of Education.

FREDERICK HERBART. (1776-1841.)

Frederick Herbart was born in Oldenburg, Germany. He was prepared for the gymnasium of his native town by his mother and a tutor. Five years later he entered the noted Jena University.

After graduation he became a teacher. He soon penetrated into the ethical and psychological truths of education. He became acquainted with and was a warm friend of the distinguished Pestalozzi. The personality and ideas of Pestalozzi greatly impressed him.

Herbart explains his conceptions of the method of Pestalozzi in a number of works. Among them are "How Gertrude Teaches her Children" and "To Three Women."

While professor in Goething University, he wrote "Outlines of Pedagogic Lectures" and "General Pedagogics," the most important of his writings.

Herbart is called the founder of scientific pedagogics. "The aim of education he derived from ethics, the ways and means from psychological laws. He made Pedagogics a department of applied science whose principles of application are founded upon psychology."

OTHER EDUCATORS.

There are many prominent teachers of the last fifty years, whose names have not yet found their place in any one work on education, but whose influence on education should be noted by modern students of pedagogy. Some of them we will consider.

Wm. T. Harris, U. S. Commissioner of Education, is one of the foremost pedagogical thinkers of to-day. He believes in development according to self-activity and that school education and all education is a delicate matter of adjustment, inasmuch as it deals with two factors, spontaneity and prescription. B. A. Hinsdale, professor of pedagogy, University of Michigan, believes that education begins with the being to be educated, that is, the child, and it culminates in his higher nature, that is, his mind. Col. Francis W. Parker, principal of Chicago normal school, is the author of the so-called Quincy method. James S. Hughes, inspector of public schools, Toronto, Ontario, is the author of Mistakes in Teaching. W. N. Hailmann, ex-superintendent of Indian education, is the author of History of Pedagogy. L. Seeley, teacher of pedagogy in normal school, Trenton, N. J., Richard G. Boone, principal of Ypsilanti normal school and author of Education in the United States, E. W. Scripture, director of psychological labaratory, Yale University, A. S. Draper, president of Illinois University, T. G. Rooper, inspector of schools, England, G. Stanley Hall president of Clark University, Charles W. Elliot, president of Harvard College are among the foremost educators of to-day.

19TH CENTURY SUMMARY.

The educational activity of the 19th century is unprecedented. It has produced remarkable results in the condition of the lower classes. The century is noted for the growth of elementary education, professional training of teachers, school supervision, manual and technical training and the numerous associations for the discussion of educational topics. Education is being organized on a psychological and scientific basis. The church and the state have been separated. All members of the human family receive the benefits of an education. Education is regarded as a social problem. A deep sentiment of humanity has been awakened—a calamity in one community awakens a deep sympathy in another.

CHAPTER XV.

COMMON SCHOOLS IN AMERICA.

Massachusetts was the first colony to make a provision by law for the benefit of common schools. This law passed in 1642. It sought to make her scholars serve the state and enjoined upon the town universal education, but did not make schooling free. The act of 1647 gave the school system of that state its birth. This made the first free schools in the world, with the exception of those in Sweden. Three years later Connecticut passed a similar act. Other New England states followed the examples of these two pioneers of free schools.

The Dutch early established schools in New Amsterdam. At the opening of the Revolution, several schools were supported in the colony. The English did not show the same interest in education that the Dutch had. In 1795 the first appropriation for common schools was made, but the common school system was not established until 1813. The schools were made free in 1849, but remained so but for a short time. They have been free since 1867.

Penn early introduced education into his colony, but later the school system was not progressive. The institution of slavery in the south interfered with popular education there.

There were no common schools south of Pennsylvania

before the revolution. Those who could afford it sent their sons across the waters for their education. There were, however, two exceptions to the above statement. The Dorchester Seminary of grammar grade was established in South Carolina in 1734 by some Massachusetts gentlemen and the Battle Creek school of like rank in Maryland.

After the American Declaration of Independence was passed, most of the American statesmen were in favor of meeting the necessity of public education. The congress of the confederation passed an act in 1785, reserving lot No. 16 of every township of the Western Territory "for the maintenance of public schools within said township." An act passed 1787 pertaining to the government of the "territory of the U. S. northeast of the river Ohio" contained the following article:, "Religion morality and knowledge being necessary to good government and the happiness of mankind, schools and the needs of education shall forever be encouraged." In 1802, Congress passed an act authorizing the states formed out of the Northwest Territory to reserve certain lands for school purposes. Similar compacts have been made with other states admitted into the Union. By act of July 23, 1787, congress ordered that when new states were formed, "not more than two complete townships be given perpetually for the purpose of a university." By act of 1862, Congress donated to each state thirty thousand acres of public land not otherwise reserved for "the support of colleges for the cultivation of agricultural and mechanical science and art." By act of 1836, Congress gave to each state thirty million dollars, the surplus in the U. S. treasury. Sixteen states used theirs for common school purposes.

Among the men who did much for popular education during the early days of our republic was Dr. Benjamin Rush, of Pennsylvania, Gen. Francis Monroe, of South Carolina, Christopher Dock, of Pennsylvania, and Chauncey Lee, of New York.

The text books early in use were Dilworth's Spelling Book, Hodder's Arithmetic, Webster's Spelling Book, Daboll's Arithmetic, Bailey's English and Latin Grammar, Lindley Murray's Grammar, Morse's Geography, Webster's Historical Reader.

By act Massachusetts established a high school in 1797. The Philadelphia high school was established in 1837, the New York Free academy in 1849.

SCHOOLS IN NEW YORK STATE.

The first official act pertaining to public education in the state was enacted by the patrons in 1629 and related to the ways and means whereby they might supply a minister and a school-master. The first regular schoolmaster, Adam Roelandsen taught school from 1633 to 1639. Private school existed in the colony during the seventeenth century. In 1687 a Latin school was opened in New York city, and in 1702 an act was passed for the "encouragement of a grammar free school in the city of New York." Columbia, (King's) college was established in 1754.

In 1784, the board of Regents of the University of the state of New York was created. In 1787, its powers were changed and much enlarged. This is the board that to-day has all matters pertaining to higher education in its hands. The Regents grant charters to colleges of the state, receive annual reports from them, admit secondary schools under their supervision and inspection and have other duties pertaining to higher education of the state. The Regents' examinations date from 1828. To distribute the literature fund more equitably, examinations in the preliminary branches were ordered by an act July 7, 1864. Since 1870 all papers have been sent to Albany for review. In June 1878, examinations were first held in advanced branches. Now, a student must hold in this state Regents' certificates of different grades to enter upon any professional course offered in the state.

Governor Clinton in his message of 1795 to the legislature called for the establishment of common schools. By the passage of this act $50,000 was annually appropriated for five years for the purpose of teaching children the branches of an English education. This measure provided for county supervision. In 1800 this act was repealed. The Lancastrian system of conducting schools came into New York about 1809. It was a system of mutual instruction. By the aid of monitors several classes could recite at the same time. The first act contemplating a permanent system of common schools was passed in 1812.

In 1812, through the recommendation of Governor Tompkins a bill providing for State aid to schools, in case the district should vote to levy by tax an equal amount was introduced in the legislature. This remained a law until 1840.

In 1813 Gideon Hawley was elected first superintendent of schools, with a salary of $300. In 1821 the superintendent's functions were given to the Secretary of State. In 1838, the district school libraries were started. The office of county superintendent was created in 1841.

The office of State superintendent was restored in 1854 with Victor M. Rice as the first occupant of the office. The Union Free School act was passed in 1853. In 1849 and 1851, acts were passed repealing the old rate-bill, but the schools were not absolutely free until 1867. From that time, schools have been supported by tax.

Among the superintendents of public instruction appear the names of Victor M. Rice, 1854; Abraham B. Weaver, 1874; Neil Gilmore, 1876; A. S. Draper, 1886; James F. Crocker, 1892; Charles R. Skinner, 1895; Under Secretary of State A. C. Flagg in 1838 district libraries were established. Training classes were organized in 1834 under the supervision of the Regents. In 1843, the first institute was held in Ithaca. In 1844 the first Normal School in the State was established in Albany with David P. Page as its principal.

In 1874 a compulsory education law was enacted. The age limits were 8 and 14 years. In 1856 the office of school commissioner was created. The first State convention of teachers in this State was held in Utica in 1830.

For the professional training of teachers the state has established several normal schools, teachers' institutes in each county annually, summer institutes, and teachers' training classes in union schools.

For the support of the schools the State has the literature fund, the common school fund, the U. S. deposit fund, free school fund and local taxes.

In 1784, the Board of Commissioners of the Land Office in this State was empowered to reserve a lot of 300 acres for the use of a minister and one of 390 for a school or schools. By an act of 1786, the Surveyor General was directed to mark one "Gospel and Schools," the other "For Promoting Literature." The first became the nucleus of various school funds; the latter the nucleus of the Literature fund. By the acts of 1790, 1801, 1819, 1827, 1831 and others of more recent date, the Literature fund distributed by the Regents for the benefit of academic and secondary schools in 1896 was $237,002.26.

The common School fund had its origin in the act of 1805. The net proceeds of 500,000 acres of unappropriated land of the State were to be used as a fund for the support of the common schools. The fund at the present amounts to about $4,000,000, the income from which is about $170,000.

The United States Deposit fund came from the national treasury. By an act of Congress, during Jackson's administration, the surplus in the treasury excepting $5,000,000 was directed to be distributed among the states. New York State's share was $4,014,520.71. This was applied to the common schools.

The Free School fund is the term applied to the money raised by State tax.

Normal Schools.—Albany normal college; normal schools at Brockport, Buffalo, Cortland, Fredonia, Geneseo, Jamaica, New Paltz, Oneonta, Oswego, Plattsburgh, Potsdam.

A few New York State Colleges.—Columbia, Union, Hamilton, Colgate, St. John's, Cornell, Vassar, Wells, St. Francis, St. Lawrence, Elmira.

APPENDIX.

THE AIM OF EDUCATION AS VIEWED BY DIFFERENT PEOPLE AND PERSONS.

Chinese: To impress traditional ideas and customs and to preserve the established order of society.
Ancient Persia: Physical strength and moral rectitude.
Ancient Hebrews: To become faithful servants of Jehovah.
Sparta: To train soldiers.
Athens: Beautiful soul in beautiful body.
Rome: To make a man fit to perform justly, skillfully and magnanimously all the offices, both public and private, of peace and war.
Socrates: To dispel error and discover truth.
Plato: To give to body and soul all the beauty and all the perfection of which they are capable.
Aristotle: Attainment of happiness through perfect virtue.
Quintilian: To make orators.
Seneca: Not for school, but for life.
Charlemagne: To make intelligent citizens.
Monastic Schools: To foster interest of the church.
Burgher Schools: To train for the practical wants of life.

Erasmus: General education to prepare for future duties.

Luther: More effective service in church and State.

Melancthon: General education for service as citizen and subject.

Sturm: Piety, knowledge, eloquence.

Montaigne: To make men before specialists.

Rabelias: To form a complete man, skilled in art and industry.

Comenius: To obtain eternal happiness in and with God through education.

Locke: Practical knowledge rather than mere learning, and a sound mind in a sound body.

Rousseau: Complete living.

Pestalozzi: Natural, progressive and systematic development of all the powers.

Froebel: To direct natural activities to useful ends.

History of Education questions for training classes prepared by the Department of Public Instruction at Albany.

JANUARY, 1896.

1 (a) Name one Greek and one Roman educator. (b) State some idea concerning education for which each was noted.
2. Name two distinguished teachers of the sixteenth century, and give a characteristic of each.
3. State some way in which the cause of education has been furthered by each of the following: Martin Luther, Thomas Arnold, Horace Mann, David Page.
4. (a) About what time were the Jesuit schools established? (b) State two characteristics that made their educational work effective.

5. Name an educational work of each of the following: Comenius, Locke, Spencer.

6. What is the title of Rousseau's great educational work? Describe briefly the early training of the principal character therein.

7. What are the principal features of the kindergarten education? What great educator is regarded as the founder of this system?

8. Give the leading facts in the life of Pestalozzi.

9. What is the oldest college in the state of New York? In what year was it founded? What was its original name?

10. In what year were the public schools of the State of New York made free? Name four important measures that have since been adopted to promote education in the state.

JUNE, 1896.

1. Characterize briefly the education of the Israelites, the Athenians, and the Romans.

2. For what is each of the following persons especially noted as educators. (a) Euclid; (b) Genke; (c) Quintilian; (d) Arnold; (e) Charlemagne.

3. Sketch the life of (a) Froebel; (b) Mann.

4. State the chief characteristics of the Renaissance. About what time did it occur?

5. Give the title of an important educational work of which was the author: Comenius, Pestalozzi, Quick, Plato, Quintilian, Spencer, Locke, Fenelon.

6. Make a brief statement showing the general character of the education during the Middle Ages.

7. With what important act in connection with the public schools of New York is the name of (a) George Clinton; (b) Andrew S. Draper? About what time did each occur?

8. State three principles enunciated by Pestalozzi.

9. Name a prominent educator of the sixteenth century, of the seventeenth, and of the eighteenth century.

10. (a) Where and about what time was the first normal school of the state established? (b) Who was its first principal and what educational book did he write? (c) Locate five other normal schools. (d) Name and locate four colleges of the state.

APPENDIX.
JANUARY, 1897.

1. Give the prominent features in the educational work of Pythagoras.
2. Mention the characteristic features of the Spartan education.
3. State some characteristic of educational work that is associated with each of the following names: Abelard, Strum, Ascham, Bacon, Montaigne.
4. What have been the successive effects of Christianity upon education?
5. Describe the monastic schools of the Middle Ages as to (a) organization; (b) science of study; (c) aims; d() discipline.
6. Compare the schools of the Jesuits and the schools of the Port Royalists as to (a) extent; (b) character of work; (c) results.
7. Mention two leading causes and two leading results of the Renaissance.
8. Mention four prominent educators of the Renaissance and give the characteristics of the educational work of any two.
9. Give a brief sketch of the career of Comenius as an educator.
10. Write a brief historical sketch of the professional training of teachers in the state of New York.

JUNE, 1897.

1. Mention the prominent characteristics of the following educators: Plato, Euclid, Plutarch.
2. (a) Into what two divisions were the Liberal Arts grouped? (b) Name the subjects included under each division.
3. Name three noted educators who lived between the seventh and fourteenth centuries and mention an educational idea, principle or theory for which each is noted.
4. Give the general characteristics of education during the period of the Renaissance.
5. What were the "teaching societies?" To what centuries was the work principally confined?
6. Give an estimate of the educational work of (a) Erasmus; (b) Sturm.
7. Who wrote Emile, Institutes of Oratory, Education of Girls, Thoughts on Education, American School Journal?
8. Name two noted English educators and mention prominent characteristics of their educational work.
9. Sketch the life of Henry Barnard as an educator.
10. What are the special functions of (a) the University of the State of New York; (b) the Department of Public Instruction.

APPENDIX.

JANUARY, 1898.

1-2. Compare the contributions of the Oriental (Asiatic) nations to the cause of education with the contributions of the ancient classical nations (Greece and Rome).
3. Name a prominent representative of (a) scholastic education; (b) humanistic education; (c) scientific or practical education.
4. Arrange the following events in order of relative importance to education and show how each influenced the Renaissance: invention of gunpowder;discovery of America; invention of printing; downfall of Constantinople.
5-6. Give an idea of the general nature and character of the following books and name the author of each: Orbis Pictus; Emile.
7. State the leading principles in the educational plan of Froebel.
8. Give a brief sketch of Erasmus as an educator.
9. Mention a prominent characteristic of the educational work of (a) Jacotot; (b) Spencer; (c) Aristotle.
10. Compare the condition of education in this state during the early part of the century with its present condition as to (a) the professional training of teachers; (b) common school education; (c) higher education.

JUNE, 1898.

1. Among what ancient people was each of the following the predominant influence on education: (a) caste; (b) tradition; (c) theocracy ?
2. Mention two respects in which the education of the Romans excelled.
3. Mention three prominent educators that lived between (a) 500 B. C. and 300 B. C.; (b) 1450 A. D. and 1600 A. D.
4. State for what each of the following men is especially noted as an educator: Euclid, Saint Jerome, Abelard, Bacon, Page.
5. Name the author of each of the following works and give the approximate time when each was written: (a) Leonard and Gertrude; (b) The Republic; (c) Gate of Tongues Unlocked (Janua Linguarum Reserata); (d) Education as a Science; (e) Novum Organum (or Insturatio Magna).
6. State and explain the effect of the Crusades on the education of the Middle Ages.
7. State three important ideas advanced by Locke in "Thoughts on Education".

APPENDIX

8. Compare the condition and character of education in the sixteenth and eighteenth centuries.
9. Mention two ways in which the National Government has directly advanced education in the States.
10. Give the names of three men that have served as Superintendent of Public Instruction in this State, and mention an important event in the administration of each.

JANUARY, 1899.

1. Describe the Socratic method of teaching and discuss its value.
2. Compare the Greek with the Roman contributions to education as to (a) extent; (b) character; (c) value.
3. Describe briefly the educational work of each of the following men, Quintilian, Melancthon, Page.
4. Describe the Port Royalist Schools as to (a) origin; (b) course of study; (c) methods; (d) results.
5. Name the authors of the following books, approximate time when written and give a general idea of its character: Republic;; How Gertrude Teaches her Children.
6. Mention two noted educators of the eighteenth century and characterize the educational work of each.
7. Name an educational treatise of which Herbert Spencer is the author, and give a general idea of its character and influence.
8. Name two prominent advocates of the study of the mother-tongue before Latin and Greek, and two of the study of Latin and Greek before the mother-tongue.
9. Describe the educational work of Horace Mann and account for its special prominence.
10. Associate with each of the following dates an important educational event in the history of the State of New York: 1784, 1795, 1805, 1813, 1834, 1843, 1844, 1867, 1889, 1895.

INDEX.

	Page.
Abelard	50
Aldhelm	49
Almagest	26
Alcuin	49
Anabasis	24
Appendix	105
Aquinas	47
Aristotle	22
Arnold	89
Asceticism	42
Ascham	62
Athenian and Spartan Ed. compared	16
Athens	13
Bacon	65
Bain	91
Barnard	95
Basedow	78
Bede	50
Benedictines	46
Charlemagne	48
Chinese	5
Colloquies	55
Comenius	66
Common schools	99
Common school funds	102
Crusades	44
Cyropædia	24
Dominicans	47

	Page.
Economics	24
Education.	
Aesthetic	13
Ancestral	5
Caste	9
Christian	39
Eighteenth Century	76, 80
During middle ages	42, 51
Greek	11
Martial	15
Nineteenth century	82
Priestly	9
Roman	29
Seventeenth century	64, 75
Sixteenth century	55, 63
Theocratic	7
Effect of Christianity on Ed	39
Emile	77
Effect of Greek Ed on Modern Ed	17
Epicurus	12
Erasmus	55
Egyptians	9
Euclid	25
Fenelon	70
Franciscans	47
Froebel	85
Grecian Education	18

INDEX

	Page.		Page.
Greeks	11	Phoenicians	10
Greecian and Roman education compared	30	Plato	20
		Pliny	35
Herbart	96	Plutarch	34
Hindoos	6	Politics	23
Humanities	53	Ptolemy	26
Inductive method	66	Pythagoras	26
Institutes of Oratory	32	Quintilian	32
Instrnatio Magna	66	Quadrivium	43
Israelities	7	Questions	106
Jacotot	88	Rabelais	59
Jansensits	73	Raitch	64
Jesuits	71	Renaissance	52
Lancastrian system	102	Republic	20
Letters to Lucilius	36	Roman Education	29
Liberal arts	43	Roman Educators	32
Locke	68	Rousseau	76
Luther	57	St. Augustine	38
Lyceum	22	St. Jerome	37
Maieutics	19	Scholasticism	53
Mann	92	Schools in N. Y. State	101
Melancthon	56	Seneca	36
Monastic schools	46	Socrates	18
Montaigne	61	Sophists	18
Natural history	35	Sparta	15
Object teaching	83	Saxony School plan	57
Oratorians	74	Spencer	90
Orbis Pictus	67	Strabo	25
Page	94	Sturm	60
Parallel lives	34	Trivium	43
Paula	37	Varro	35
Pestalozzi	82	Xenophon	24
Port-Royalists	73		

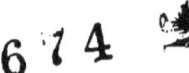